P9-DGT-900

entering the world
of the small church

a guide for leaders

Anthony G. Pappas

An Alban Institute Publication

The Publications Program of The Alban Institute is assisted by a grant from Trinity Church, New York City.

Library of Congress Catalog Card Number 88-71623
ISBN #1-56699-030-0

CONTENTS

ACKNOWLEDGMENTS

I would like to say Thank You to the many friends who have been a part of the process of nurturing this book from an idea dimly perceived to a reality. Thanks to Stan Gaede, professor of sociology at Gordon College, for connecting me with the tools I needed and seeing the promise in my first rendition; to John Wilson, professor of church history at Pittsburgh Theological Seminary, this is the book you kept telling me I should write; to Celia Hahn for her contagious enthusiasm; to Eleanor Long who must by now have the equivalent of a Ph.D in cryptology for deciphering my handwriting; to Sue Purdy for outsmarting our computer; to the Ohio State Council of Churches, Town and Country Department, which gave me the forum to first test these ideas; to my wife Cindy for her many kinds of support; to my children Rebecca and Jason whose desire to know how it was coming helped it to be; and to all the fine people who are the First Baptist Church of Block Island, were it not for you I would probably be an unhappy large church pastor somewhere in Outer Suburbia.

Tony Pappas

Grateful acknowledgment is made for use of the following: Excerpt from *Traits of a Healthy Family*, by Dolores Curran, published by Harper and Row, San Francisco, CA, 1983. Used by permission of author.

Passages from *Return to Laughter*, by Eleanor Smith Bowen, published by Harper and Row, New York, 1954. Used by permission of author.

Excerpt from "The Ghosts of Our Ancestors," in *Primitive Worlds: People Lost in Time*, by Elman R. Service. Copyright National Geographic Society, 1973. Used by permission of author.

Excerpt from *Amish Society*, by John A. Hostetler, 3rd ed. The Johns Hopkins University Press, Baltimore/London, 1980, pp 285-6. Used by permission.

Passages from "The Folk Society," by Robert Redfield, published by The American Journal of Sociology, LII:4, Jan. 1947, published by The University of Chicago Press, Chicago, IL. Used by permission.

CHAPTER I

The Small Church World

For a long while I didn't know there was a small church world.

I grew up in a small church. Spent every Sunday morning, most Sunday nights, many Wednesday nights there. Went to church picnics and suppers, youth group and missionary meetings. Knew everybody and couldn't get away with much because everybody knew me (or at least who I belonged to). Memorized my Bible verse on the way to Sunday School and vowed to follow Jesus anywhere (except overseas). Was glad I was saved (made seven trips down the aisle, till I was sure), but sad that my Congregational schoolmates weren't going to heaven with me. Yep, I grew up in a small church. But the town was small, and the outlook was small, so the church didn't seem any smaller than anything else. It was just church.

Then I went off to college. This was not applauded by the deacons who firmly believed that thinking was the root of all evil. (In this they were half right, as we shall see). However, my parents were very supportive, believing that any schooling was preferable to the school of hard knocks in which they were still enrolled. The ticket out lay along the track of education. In college I was well trained. I learned to think logically and analytically. I learned that the knottiest problems could be chopped up into little pieces (which made it much easier to sweep them under the rug). I learned that all problems have solutions (but it took much longer to realize that all solutions have problems). I learned that nothing has to be the way it is; everything can be improved. (In other words, nothing is sacred.) I learned about the history of progress and the progress of history. I thought I was taking courses, but I learned a way of thinking about life. And I learned that with a college degree it is easy to get into seminary.

Then I went to seminary. There I learned again everything I had learned in college, though now in reference to the church. I learned how to be a professional church leader, how to administer the church, how to organize the Kingdom, and how to assimilate new members. I learned about the early church and late church members (symptomatic: compensatory behavior for maternal deprivation during their infantile period). I learned the theology of the funeral service, and I attended a funeral service for theology. I learned that God is dead (but I thought this exaggerated). I learned about the church universal and, through the divinely inspired case study method, the church particular. I learned about churches with get-up-and-go, California churches a-go-go, and churches which did not pass go (nor collect the $200 from the every member canvass).

Then I got my own church and got vertigo. In January 1976 my bride of a year and a half and I moved out to Block Island, Rhode Island. I had been called to become the fulltime pastor of the First Baptist Church, a congregation which traces its roots back to 1661 and the same quest for religious freedom which motivated Roger Williams. Block Island (named for Dutch explorer Adrian Block) is ten miles out to sea off the southern coast of Rhode Island. (Overseas ministry after all.) At that time it claimed 500 residents. (Although it was alleged that in order to qualify for Revenue Sharing— available to communities of 500 or more—the local census takers had had to take a detour through the cemetery.) The Harbor Church—nicknamed for its location—gathered about two dozen for business meeting, three dozen for worship, and four dozen for covered dish suppers! Into the hands of these folk we placed ourselves—along with all our earthly possessions (which didn't fill a modestly sized U-Haul)—as the ferry boat steamed away. Never have we had reason to regret our commitment.

Two realities have emerged as determinative for me in this parish (not to mention the community). The first was obvious and immediate. We were loved. Maybe this parish was filled with "lovers." Maybe the parish had despaired of obtaining a fulltime, young pastor and so I was perceived as a God-send. Maybe we were seen as two lost, little kids—as one parishioner later described us—and we evoked pity. Maybe God went ahead and prepared the way. Whatever the reason, the kindness, concern and care toward us were palpable: Tea at a parishioner's after that first, violent boat ride. A deacon dropping by when it started "breezing up" (it blew 110 mph that day!) to make sure we were "tight." Casseroles, house plants, seed packets—evidences of country kindness. Pay raises each year, even if modest, meant to say, "You're appreciated." Parishioners who laughed at my sermonic jokes; others who didn't but would defend to the death my inability to tell them! And always, always the feeling of loyalty, of people who would be there when you needed them. We were loved.

If love was the first reality, learning was the second. But it emerged more slowly. And I almost missed it. It arose first as confusion, frustration, dissonance. It had its visible manifestations. The clothes, for example, which I had so carefully purchased on a seminarian's budget to try to fit into my suburban field education parish hung unused in one end of my closet, while my flannel shirts became threadbare through constant use. But it took me longer to take off my mental clothes. The new attire came in unexpected ways.

For example, our church sign. Our building is not easily distinguished as a church building since it is an appropriated Victorian hotel with a sanctuary wing stuck on. It seemed logical to me that in order to attract new members, and visitors, guests, drop-ins, etc., we should identify ourselves as a church. The Trustees hemmed and hawed and finally decided we needed a church business meeting to decide. What I thought would be a cut and dry vote turned into a raging debate. I brilliantly held up the sign side in an opening statement, but rapidly lost ground, primarily because I couldn't make a lick of sense out of the opposing comments. It was only years later that I realized the logic of the opposition: those who need a sign to know where the church is aren't enough a part of us to be church with us. (I understand there is a tombstone, circa 1882, in Hartford, Connecticut which reads:

Those who cared for him while living will know whose body is buried here. To others it does not matter.

So you see the situation changes, but the attitude remains the same.)

Or consider pledging. Closing the year in the black was always touchy business in our parish. Our treasurer had devised certain "tricks" to help out. (I realized this in retrospect.) One was to withhold certain types of receipts (e.g., bank interest) from reporting. This made our situation appear even worse than it was. This appearance motivated parishioners, including the treasurer herself, to give more! Thus we were, each and every year, near bankruptcy from August to December. But somehow, miraculously, we would finish the year a few dollars to the good. Once I caught on, I tired of this approach. Wouldn't it be more businesslike, straightforward and dependable to have a pledging system, I argued to our Trustees. Impossible, they answered. Why? I queried. Because we are all farmers and fishermen and we never know what kind of year we will have; we give as we can, they answered. I was too stunned to reply. Yes, they gave as they could, but not one parishioner made their living farming or fishing, nor had any since the hurricane destroyed the entire fishing fleet and most of the barns in 1938!

Or consider mission. Mission is to me a matter of individual commitment and discipline. Christ is active in the world and to the degree of my ability, opportunity and faithfulness, I support His mission in its totality. Foreign mission and local mission differ in geography but not in essence. One I support through dollars and prayers, the other through blood, sweat and tears, but they are qualitatively the same. It's just that one is close at hand. But not so for my deacons. Once I raised for their consideration a new denominational mission offering. Their concern was significant—but it was concern to protect the congregation from this offering/program! So concerned were they that they pledged money as individual deacons in order to prevent a general appeal! To them mission was ministry: local, personal, face to face. And resources were limited and small. Stewardship consisted in not wasting the group's effort to care for its own!

So you see I had entered the small church world. But I didn't know it then. I was just confused and frustrated. My initial reaction was to attribute madness/badness. To the degree that these people opposed me and my position, they were lousy Christians or nuts or both. Fortunately, a third alternative emerged by God's grace and my parishioners' patience. This third alternative was that they were operating out of a different system than I was—a system with different values, perceptions and understandings. In short, they had a different view of the world. The world looked different to small church people and their thought processes regarding it differed from my abstract, rational, educated, individualized, goal-setting point of view. This world view is not right (moral, Christian, Biblical) just because they use it, just as it is not wrong just because it differed from mine. However, if it is to be "righted," it must be changed from the inside. And if we are to minister effectively in the small church, we must first step into that world. After all, Jesus stepped into ours.

This book is offered as a first draft of a road map of the small church world.

Welcome.

But I warn you: as you journey, your perspective of the small church world will proceed from frustration to quaintness, to satisfaction, to significance, to eternity. In the end you will no longer be interested in becoming an Executive Minister, District Superintendent, Stated Clerk, Bishop, or even Executive Director of The Alban Institute!

The following section presents from an external perspective a model with which to understand the small church as a separate social and theological entity. The next section attempts "to get inside the head" of a small church person and see the world as he or she sees it. The last two sections suggest attitudes and actions for effective leadership in this small church world.

CHAPTER II

A Small Church Model—Theory and Theology

The story is told of six blind friends in India. They could scarcely conceal their excitement for they had heard that an elephant would be brought to their village that day. Among themselves they discussed what an elephant must be like for though they had heard much about elephants they never experienced one first hand. Along the roadside they waited. Upon seeing them, the kindly elephant owner stopped his massive beast and invited the blind men to come and learn what an elephant was like. The six blind men rushed forward until they made contact with the great animal. The first blind man grabbed onto the elephant's trunk. "Ah," said he, "an elephant is like a great snake." The second happened upon the tusk of the elephant. "So," he said, "an elephant is like a smooth spear." The third bumped into the elephant's leg and hugging it for support concluded, "An elephant is like the trunk of a great tree." The fourth reached up and felt the elephant's ear. "Now I know," he said, "an elephant is like the huge fan Rajahs use to keep cool." The fifth walked into the enormous torso of the animal and knew beyond the shadow of a doubt that an elephant is like a fortress wall—broad, tall and inpenetrable. The sixth latched onto the elephant's tail. "Yes. I can see now why an elephant so impresses everyone. He is like a rope which swings freely—traveling wherever it wills."

Imagine the argument the six blind friends got into that evening! Our models of reality are very powerful in determining our actions and our satisfactions. The world around us is far too complex for us to "rediscover" it each day. So we each have an operational model of reality in our heads. In order to function we each act as if the vast world around us is like unto something which we have experienced and have stored in our minds as a picture, image, model or even emotion. We are not always conscious of these models. In fact, we seldom are. They come to our awareness when things don't seem to be adding up right, when the world seems to be out of whack. At these points we receive insight into our operational models, and also have the opportunity to change them in light of a greater reality. As the six blind friends discovered, models can be "true" as far as they go. But a model is not equal to the reality it is used to convey. So there can be no 100% right model. Seminary professor Paul Minear in his book, *Image of the Church in the New Testament*[1], describes the models the New Testament authors used to depict the church—all 96 of them!! Different models have different degrees of helpfulness, though. In the sciences, models are thought to be helpful if they are 1) broadly applicable, and 2) capable of predicting further facts and relationships. As we think about the church we would like to go further. Theological models ought to be 3) true to the Biblical revelation and 4) appropriate to real people in specific societies and eras.

Some Historical Models of the Church

The church has always had a tendency to see itself in the image of the predominant social reality of its day. It might not be too bald to say that Augustine saw the Holy People of God in light of the power and organization of the Roman Empire. His thinking went a long way toward legitimizing in the minds of Christians that unholy hybrid known as the Holy Roman Empire.

Aquinas saw his heavenly Lord as like unto his experience of earthly lords, and so the church was saddled with a feudal and hierarchical ecclesiology for half a millenium.

In contrast to that model, Calvin and the Reformers saw individual election as the primary reality. The social structure was vitally significant but derivative from that reality. In this position they articulated theologically what was already happening socially and economically—the ascent of the "burghers." So intimately connected was this theology with the new social structuring that the word "protestant" and the phrase "work ethic" have become one in modern usage.

Today also we tend to understand the church in light of the predominant social reality—corporate America. Churches produce a product to meet a need on the market place. Those with inferior products (for example, "folksy" sermons, off-key choirs, spotty programming, modest physical plants often in disrepair, i.e., the small church) go bankrupt and die. This is the proper result of Adam Smith's free enterprise system. The invisible hand strikes down inefficient and archaic small churches, while prospering the corporate church. The corporate church differentiates its product from other brand names, uses long-term planning cycles, employs a marketing strategy, and sees growth as its overall criterion of success. (And, as we have recently been made all too aware, it is able to provide its C.E.O. with unbelievable "perks"—dollars, jets, condos, and even sex!)

All such societal images of the church are spiritually suspect. Some have a modicum of truth. Some are satanic. None should be used uncritically. Yet it is our natural tendency to do just that! Societal models are second nature to us. Yet the model of the church which we employ will determine, to a large degree, our faithfulness. So it behooves us as Christians to be judicious in our choice of ecclesiastical models.

Two Biblical Models of the Church

There are many, many models of the church and God's people in the Scriptures—by Minear's count 96 in the New Testament alone! But to my mind there are two that stand out as being particularly helpful to our understanding today because they are such fundamental and rich concepts. The first is the image of "the people of God." This theme recurs throughout the Biblical writings. Deuteronomy 7:6f provides us with a most insightful instance. "For you are a people holy to the Lord your God. The Lord your God has chosen you out of all the peoples on the face of the earth to be his people, his treasured possession . . . because the Lord loves you." The term "people" is not used in this passage in the same way in which it is used in modern English. It is not a reference to an aggregation of individual human beings. Rather it is being used of a coherent social entity, an ethnic grouping. In sociological and anthropological jargon it is a "folk society."

The term "folk society" was coined by anthropologist Robert Redfield.[2] (It will be described further in chapters three and four.) His idea, written in a 1947 *American Journal of Sociology* article, was to create a spectrum upon which existing societies could be sequenced and so compared in a systematic way. At each end of this societal spectrum Redfield posited an "ideal type." At one end he located the type of society of his own experience—Western, urbanized, technologically advanced, highly educated, highly mobile, based on contractual social bonds, etc. On the opposite end he placed the Folk Society, an extrapolation of the characteristics of the societies he encountered doing anthropological field work in Central America. Characteristics of the Folk Society include the following nineteen qualities:

A Folk Society is composed of a group of people who, 1) are small in number, 2) have a long-term association, 3) know each other well, and 4) have a strong sense of belonging. The group is 5) isolated from other groups in neighboring areas and conversely has a 6) high identification with the territory it occupies. It often functions as if it is 7) "in a little world off by itself." There is a strong 8) coincidence of wisdom, prestige and authority with the age of the individual which is enhanced by the fact that 9) each generation goes through a similar sequence of life events. There is a 10) simplicity of roles, 11) a primacy of oral over written communications, and a 12) straightforward level of technology. 13) The individual's position in the folk society determines his or her rights and duties, 14) behavior is as much expressive as it is effective, and 15) relationships are ends in themselves not a means of achieving an external object. 16) Social recognition in the Folk Society is a greater motivator of behavior than material gain. 17) Qualities which contribute to stability, not change, over time are valued. 18) Tradition determines actions and 19) moral worth attaches to the traditional way of doing things. The term "folk society" and those nineteen specific qualities serve to objectify what we might loosely call "a tribe."

So in everyday talk the word "tribe" comes closest to the meaning of the Biblical "people." The Biblical author proclaims that God is making for himself a people, a tribe, a society in which his glory and holiness can be reflected. So it is that Peter writes of the church, "You are a chosen race, a royal priesthood, a holy nation, God's own people, that you may declare the wonderful deeds of him who called you out of darkness into his marvellous light. Once you were no people but now you are God's people." (I 2:9-10) It is entirely consistent with the Scriptures, then, to picture the church as God's tribe. As such, God's people are rightly to have their own language and culture, history and traditions, patriarchs and heroes, stories and legends, Indians and chiefs, institutions and ways of doing things. The church is to be a society distinguishable from other societies and one which demands total allegiance and participation. Though this is not always realized, it is still "in the nature of things."

The second model may at first glance appear to vary significantly from the first. It may even seem contradictory, but it is in fact complementary. Where the first takes an external perspective and sees God's people as an entity, the second looks at the internal life and functioning of the church and sees it in terms of its parts and their relationships. This second model depicts the church as the "Body of Christ." Paul writes to the church in Rome, "We, though many, are one body in Christ, and individually members one of another. Having gifts that differ according to the grace given to us, let us use them . . . let love be genuine . . . love one another with brotherly affection; outdo one another in showing honor." (12:4-10) Here and in the other "Body" passages in I Corinthians and Ephesians, Paul is concerned with the dynamics which are to characterize the internal life of God's people. Love and deference are to be the attitudes with which Christians relate to one another. Mutuality and complementarity are to be the ways Christians live together. Here individuality is a means to enhance the whole church, not an end to itself. The emotion evoked is a family feeling: one is to feel and act toward the church the way one does toward one's own family.

Two Models of the Church Current Today

A half dozen years ago, I determined that my parish needed to grow, develop and progress. I went to my local Christian bookstore and came home laden with books from seminary professors, successful (read: large) church pastors, and denominational officials each explaining in great detail how one can get one's church moving. I sat myself down to learn from these people. I learned all about systems theory, mission statements, goal setting and strategizing. I learned about resource analysis, writing objectives and managing by them. I learned about long range planning and one minute managing. I learned about flow charts and force field analysis.

In the end, I learned that the church thinks of itself as if it were a business. In this organizational approach the church is seen as any other organization. It is seen as a thing, created by its management, brought into being by their decisions and behaviors. It is rational. That is to say that there is a logical connection between its behaviors and its desired outputs. It is structured. That is to say that the relationships between component parts and the procedures which are employed to accomplish the task of the organization are determined by the mind of management, and explicitly formulated, so much so that they are subject to being captured in an operating manual. It is bureaucratic. This is not to say that it is necessarily tangled up in red tape, but that it works through a hierarchy with clear chains of command and responsibility, and that what is valued is an *orderly* method of accomplishing the task. It is task oriented. That is to say that it exists to get a job done even when that job is fellowship (so churches train deacons to organize and shepherd cell groups). It is energy consuming. That is to say that the organization cannot continue to function at its present level unless it receives massive inputs of resources. These resources are in terms of people, property, time, effort, skills and dollars. In this business or organizational model, the church is thus understood.

I find this business model of the church theologically nauseating. It is true that any grouping of human beings that exists over time has some form and degree of organization. Therefore the organizational approach will have some validity. But this model serves only at the lowest level of understanding the church. The church, even the simplest and smallest church, has something more than this organizational aspect to its nature. It has, somehow in some way, the living presence of God in it and upholding it. This living aspect must be accounted for. So I prefer a biological to a business model. In my understanding the church is more organism than organization. In this model the church is not seen as a thing created by the will of its managers. It is the living Body of Christ created by the loving intention of the Lord of all life. It is not primarily rational. Of course, its by-laws may be logical and its committee work efficient. But it really lives on a much deeper level. It lives on the level of shared experience, of tradition and even habit. Its thinking exists to serve this deeper level of being. This church is not essentially structure, it is essentially process. It is alive. It grows and shares and moves through the events and the flow and the sequence of life. Of course it has a structure, but this structure is, like a pipe, a conduit for the really important things which flow through it, the loving relationships with one another and with the God who makes them possible. It is not essentially hierarchical. It has means of accomplishing things but these are more personal, mutual and habitual. People do things much more than offices, committees and task forces. It is not primarily task oriented. It is primarily relationally oriented. It may do a lot of things, but its real goal is simply to be together, to fellowship, to share life—you might almost say, to play. And it is more energy neutral or energy creating, than it is energy consuming. Large inputs, especially large pastoral inputs, are seldom necessary to assure its continuation and even its health. It keeps going with some kind of almost indescribable inertia, muddling through but enjoying its life.

The business model and the biological model may be opposed to each other as alternative understandings of the church. But the biological model is really not one model but a cluster of models. The family is a traditional and very rich model of the church and the small church in particular. Dr. Harold Moore,[3] of the Center for Career Development and Ministry, Newton, Massachusetts, has written recently comparing the small church to a family system. He sees parallels between kinds of small churches and kinds of families. He sees the sequences that churches go through as parallel to those of families over time. And he sees the dynamics within small churches as like unto family dynamics (e.g., the "symptom bearer"). Duncan McIntosh[4] has developed a classification of churches according to family type by which he believes he can predict the future movement of a particular church. These are the constricted family type church which resembles a tightly bound nuclear family and which is unlikely to grow over time, the restricted family type church which resembles a family of siblings which will experience some growth over time, and a reproducing family type church which resembles an extended family of cousins which is able to experience high growth over time. Prof. Maynard Hatch of Central Baptist Seminary has been working with churches in a field placement setting using certain characteristics of a healthy family to measure the "temperature" (degree of health) in the church situation. He focuses on the fifteen familial qualities described in Dolores Curran's book, *Traits of a Healthy Family*.[5] "The healthy family

1. communicates and listens
2. affirms and supports one another
3. teaches respect for others
4. develops a sense of trust
5. has a sense of play and humor
6. exhibits a sense of shared responsibility
7. teaches a sense of right and wrong
8. has a strong sense of family in which rituals and traditions abound
9. has a balance of interaction among members
10. has a shared religious core
11. respects the privacy of one another
12. values service to others
13. fosters family table time and conversation
14. shares leisure time
15. admits to and seeks help with problems."

A second model in the living category is given by Carl Dudley. He sees the small church as a "single cell of caring people."[6] By analogy one can speak of a concentrated nucleus where the "hereditary" and determinative qualities are located, a broader "sea" in living contact with the whole, and a high but permeable boundary with its greater environment. Because of these living and intense qualities, Dudley speaks of pastoral leadership in the small church more as "lover" than "manager."

We move next to what I call the "medley models." These are a series of models of the church which vary according to the size of the church. Arlin J. Rothauge in his booklet *Sizing Up a Congregation*[7] classifies churches in four categories: the family church (up to 50 members), the pastoral church (50–150), the program church (150–350), and the corporation church (350 and up). In *Looking in the Mirror*,[8] Lyle Schaller depicts churches according to the average number in worship. If there are fewer than 35, he likens the church to a cat, 35–100 is like a collie dog, 100–175 is like a garden, 175–225 is like a house, 225–450 is like a mansion, 450–700 is like a ranch, and over 700 is like a whole nation! These models are very interesting for their variety, creativity and specificity, but they obtain these qualities at the cost of an overall model of the church.

Now I would like to propose a model of the church, and especially the small church. I propose that we think of the small church as a society, but a particular kind of society. That is the "Folk Society" to which we referred earlier. In other words, to my mind the best model of the small church is to understand it as a tribe. This model is thoroughly Biblical as we have seen. But it is not only that it is contained in the Bible. This model is fundamental to understanding the dynamics of God's action in the Old Testament and the hope of God's people in the New Testament. From the call of Abraham to the heavenly predictions of Revelations, God has been working to make real exactly this type of society. This is our Biblical origin and our spiritual hope. Secondly, this model is explanative. From my own experience (although a full description would require another book!), I have come to see that those behaviors, values and perspectives in my small church which so frustrated my rational and goal oriented approach are thoroughly explicable in terms of folk society life. In fact they are predictable. And this is a third reason for putting forward this model: it is most helpful in predicting behaviors and responses and as a guide for discerning which leadership acts will be functional, meaningful and satisfying.

What are some of the specifics of this tribal approach? The first is the realization that roles more than offices determine the social landscape. So much has been made of some of these roles elsewhere that I need do no more than list them here. There are patriarchs and matriarchs, elders, chiefs and witch doctors, gatekeepers and scapegoats, and the elderly story tellers as well as the group of gossipers who create the stuff of future stories! And the list could be made much longer, but the important thing to remember is that it is these types of roles which are really important not the rational structuring which pastors usually think is important.

Secondly, what holds a tribe and a church together is commitment not favorable cost-benefit ratios. The social bond is covenant not contract. The members understand their own well being in terms of the well being of the whole, and they are in it for the long run. It is their life. The little boy who responded to an inquiry after carrying his injured sibling up a hill to home with, "He ain't heavy, he's my brother" sums it up very nicely.

A third characteristic of tribal society concerns the priority of social connections. A wise businessman will hire an outside consultant or sub out a job as is appropriate and economic. The outsider is not to the businessman an enemy per se, but a potentially positive resource to be utilized as is expeditious. Nothing could be further from the truth for a tribe. The outsider is an enemy almost by definition. Not knowing who we are and how we do things puts the outsider beyond the history and social interaction which gives meaning to the tribal world and its members. The outsider is an alien presence, like a pebble in one's shoe, irritating, a deviation from the correct order of the world. How often are first time small church pastors puzzled by the lack of enthusiasm in the congregation for their evangelization plans and the frequent outright dismay when they succeed in bringing new people in! It is not only those new folk he brings into the church who are outsiders, but even the pastor himself who is initially, at least, an outsider to the ways and mores of his small church. The problem of integration is not limited to small churches, though. In the business model, the newcomer is integrated rationally through a "New Members Class" or socially by a placement in a subgroup of the church. In a tribe, a newcomer would be likely to be initiated by listening around the campfire. After a while the tribe's stories will become his stories, and the tribe's way of doing and seeing things will become his way. For most small churches today, the campfire has been replaced by the covered dish supper, but the function is the same.

Then there is the issue of the focus of concern. Businesses are vitally concerned about any aspect of the environment that will affect their well being and profitability. New government regulations, the prime rate, potential interruptions in raw material supply, consumer preference shifts, labor demands—all of these things draw the attention and the action of the business corporation. The church with its self image drawn from the business world has its attention similarly focused on its environment. World missions, third world relief, social action, denominational politics, demographic patterns, new member recruitment—these are the types of things that concern such a church. The tribal church cares about certain aspects of its environment, but the main focus of its concern is internal. What is going on with those in its social world is the issue of most importance. So the endless prelude to every board meeting—who is in the hospital, who is pregnant, whose cousin dropped in from *Oshkosh* to visit. Wasted time to every goal oriented pastor, but crucially important to those in the clan type church.

The attention and action of the business corporation regarding its environment is often expressed as an attempt to keep its future options open. The corporation is trying to position itself in relation to the future. The last thing it wants to do is find itself in a dead end position without opportunities to change things. The tribe on the other hand does not really care for options. What the tribe desires is continuity. It wants tomorrow to look like yesterday. Life is, in general terms, the way it ought to be. What is important is to live it out, not change it. Jockeying in order to position oneself among possible future options is a peculiar, if not incomprehensible, exercise. Where we have been is where we want to go. The patterns of our life are a given. God has established them, we are to live them out.

Each of these characteristics of the folk society model has implications for leadership in the small church. Many of these implications run counter to the prevailing wisdom (the predominant society model). Nevertheless, if the tribal model is more true to the reality of God's church, then it should be our touchstone for faith, understanding and action as we seek to serve our God today in the small church.

Now let us enter the world of the small church.

CHAPTER III

An Inside Look at the Small Church World

The Relation of Thought and Action in a Social System

Thought and Action. That they go together is obvious. But how? That is not quite so clear. Since even to ask the question is a mental exercise, the presumption of longstanding is that we think and on that basis act. We desire something and we exert ourselves to accomplish that end. We envision something new and we expend effort and energy to bring it into being.

While this is so true to our experience that few would deny it, its value has been questioned of late. In fact, the opposite position has gained currency in recent years. That is, that the relationship between thought and action runs more from action to thought than vice versa. Understanding follows behavior. When people act a certain way they soon come to understand that as the right way to act. The map in our minds is much less a chart to our future than it is a description of our present limitations.

Who is right—those who claim thought leads to action or those who claim action leads to thought? This chicken and egg controversy, I submit, is actually a red herring. It is irrelevant whether the chicken or the egg came first. What is important for us to know is that in our experience the one leads to the other in an ongoing sequence of life and productivity. Thought and action are related to each other in a continuous process of cause and effect, of occurrence and response, of event and reaction. So our mental map of the world leads us to act in certain ways which in turn reinforce or reinterpret our mind's chart which in turn leads to further action and so on.

Further, the individual's thought and his or her group's behavioral norms form a whole. That is, we tend to act in ways that "fit" with our understanding of the world. And we understand the world in ways that "fit" with the way in which the world is played out around us. There develops over time a congruency between the thought patterns of the individual and the behavioral patterns of his social world. It is not just that deviation from the standards of the group (e.g., backbiting) are punished (confrontation and rebuke). It is that the very way in which one thinks about the world is shaped by the social group of which he or she is a part.

This may seem obvious. And yet it is my experience that this wholeness, this connection between one's thought and one's world, is almost totally overlooked in the current "wisdom" on church renewal. This is particularly a problem for the small church. For those who write (often large church pastors, seminary professors, denomination officials) tend to live in a different world from their small church brothers and sisters. Their thoughts on church renewal, faithfulness and health are foreign to a small church person, for the two think differently. I certainly am not claiming that the small church is, in and of itself, perfect, complete and faithful. What I am saying is that in order for us to understand how we can encourage the small church to be all that God intended it to be, we need to understand how the small church thinks, how it perceives its world, and how it normally acts within that world. The thought/action system of the small church varies significantly from that of other institutions. We may call the thought patterns of small church people a "folk mentality." For it is closer to the thinking of people in "folk societies" than to the thinking of people in complex, bureaucratic and abstract organizations, as we shall see.

Seeing the World as a Totality

"Just another manic Monday, I wish it were Sunday." So a pop song laments the beginning of another work week. For the American worker there are two times, even two worlds, in each week. There is the Monday through Friday working week. Time is put in. Money is earned. Maybe, if one is lucky, careers are advanced. Then there is the weekend. For some this is real life. It may only be that the gin mill is substituted for the treadmill, but the change is greatly valued. Leisure is a boom industry in our society. That is where it is at. Some people will come right out and say, "I live for the weekend." On whether this is good or bad, I have my own thoughts. But that for these people, millions in our society, the world is fractured, broken in half, is beyond debate. In fact, it is impossible to speak meaningfully about their life as a whole. Their life is not whole. It is composed of a series of discrete lives. Work life (8 AM–5 PM, Monday–Friday). Play life (evenings and weekends). Church life (I have one friend who values highly an intense fellowship group he is a part of in a large, urban church—yet he never sees any of the other members outside of the group meetings). Family life. Social life (frequently the residue of an elaborate screening process in which only those who are "like us" remain). Those various lives can add up to a busy week, but, of themselves, they are separate and discrete.

In this arrangement we do not expect to have any significant level of overlap between "lives." In fact, it can be downright disorienting to have a person from one's work life show up in one's church or social life. A connection like that complicates the neatness of the compartmentalized life. Sometimes it is tolerated. Sometimes the person acts to restore the separation ("Dealing with him all day at work is enough. I am not going to sit next to him at worship, too.")

Compare this view of life to what happens in my town. I have pastored the First Baptist Church of Block Island, an eleven square mile island ten miles off the Rhode Island coast, for over a decade. There are 600 or so of us who live here year round. (There is a large group of seasonal people also, but we don't count them.) Of the 600, I can place nearly everyone by name or face or connection. ("He's Maggie's boy friend." "Oh, he's worked for Billy now for two weeks. Didn't you know?") And it is certainly not because I am pastor that I know nearly everyone. Everyone knows everyone. In fact, I am probably one of the last to know "the latest" because I am not in the grapevine directly. (I don't own a CB, nor do I hang around the Post Office parking lot!) Should a new person come to worship there is an immediate effort during the coffee hour which follows to place him—the bold, by introducing themselves to the stranger, and the shy, by checking with the pastor, "Who's that?" (Note: This desire to avoid a lacuna in the social chart of the parish should not be confused with a welcoming in Christian love—that may or may not be involved also!) A typical day may find my going from exercise to my office, to the grocery store, the post office, the gas station, picking up my daughter at school, attending a committee meeting, and going out to dinner (at a parishioner's). Throughout this day I am not likely to encounter anyone whom I don't already know. The cast of characters in my work, leisure, social, etc., lives varies only slightly. So my world may have different facets, but it is essentially a unity, a totality. Some may consider this confining and limiting—as in some ways it is—but I consider it a structure for growth. For in this kind of world, I am unable to run away from my interpersonal difficulties.

Some years ago my stance on a school issue offended a teacher and his wife. Their response was to snub me in public. It hurt me (a sensitive soul!) to have my "hello" or hand wave returned with a glare or a quickly turned head. Because I could not avoid running into them in the course of daily life, I had to figure out what to do. I determined to live by my standards not their response. So I continued to be friendly—sometimes, I admit to my shame, exaggeratedly so as I seemed to cope better if I made it a game. But after a while came a nod, a muttered "Hi." Then when sickness came, I went to visit and was received. They resumed coming to church. Over the course of the illness, my visits were received with genuine warmth. In the end, I was asked to conduct the funeral service and my tears were sincere and my efforts appreciated by the spouse. I grew up a bit, because I had nowhere to run, except away from my own immaturity. This world is a totality.

And it is unitary in a time sense, too. The routine of life is daily, not weekly. The week divides into weekdays and weekends more on the calendar than in our experience. A while back I was assisting an engineer in testing for the water table on a lot my wife and I hoped to build our "dream" house (that is, our own home) on some day. He was working at an amazing rate. "Why?" I asked. His boss had said that this was his last job for the week. He smelled a long weekend and so he was hurrying to get back to where he could enjoy himself. His behavior made me think about myself and my fellow islanders. Little new or different happens on the weekend for us. Most of us work for ourselves. No clocks to be punched. What work remains to be done hangs over our heads twenty-four hours a day, seven days a week. Fishermen launch out according to the weather not the day of the week. In the summer the island works seven days straight out every week. In the off season it winds down or gears up. In ten plus years as pastor I have yet to establish a regular day off—not that I am not interested in one, but the parishioners don't comprehend why one would take a day off from (not work, but) life. Life has its ebbs and flows, but they are daily and annual. They reflect, in fact, the very flow of nature. They are natural, integrated and form a whole.

Life is unitary and global. Its movements constitute a oneness. This wholeness is inherently satisfying and is "felt" as right and normal. Gaps and breaks in one's knowledge of the whole are problematic. People are motivated to "fill in the gaps." This enterprise is a (maybe *the*) major "work" of small church people. This is frequently much to the consternation of the pastor whose sights are set on the bringing in of the Kingdom. Instead, those present at the Deacons' Board or the Governing Committee seem to be engaged in a con-

spiracy to avoid the pastor's programmatic agenda. Who's sick?
Who's pregnant? Who's going to and coming back from college?
Who's facing moving to a nursing home? These questions constitute
the basic agenda of small church people. The answers to these
questions renew our world. The holes are plugged. The gaps are
filled in. My world is whole again. Now, pastor, was there anything
on your mind?

No Need to Reinvent the Wheel

Life in the small church is also understood as a totality because it
doesn't change much over time. Life is recurrent. It is a sequence of
issues, circumstances and requirements that are essentially repeti-
tious. A behavioral response, though arbitrary, once in place, becomes a true solution. It is a true solution in that it meets or at least
addresses the problem and, therefore, liberates one to concern oneself about other things in life. Or to be at peace. Life is not able to
be totally resolved. Bringing into question a behavioral pattern (a
solution), no matter how irrational that pattern seems from an outside perspective or has become due to the changes caused by the
passage of time, is frequently perceived as a disruption in our familiar world.

"Okay, now that we have agreed that each of you wants to teach
the same Sunday School class as last year, let's turn our attention to
Sunday School rooms—which class should meet in which room,"
said Suzie, the new wife of Bill Prescott. Bill grew up in Poplar
Knolls Community Church, was missed while away at the state agri-
cultural college, and is now "back home," running his Dad's farm
and resuming his place in the life of his church. Suzie was welcomed in as a new member of the church family. After a year of
doing a good job as a Sunday School teacher, she was invited to
become chairman of the Christian Education Committee and she accepted, much to the relief of the aged incumbent who had long felt
that she had done her turn and it was time for younger blood to
take over. "I've tried to figure this out," Suzie continued. "The
larger classes should meet in the larger rooms, and—"

"Except that the largest class isn't the largest class," chimed in
Allan, long term teacher of the rambunctious fourth, fifth and sixth
graders. "The largest class in enrollment is the Sr. Highs, but if two
or three come, it's a banner Sunday. My class is third largest in enrollment but we get a bigger turnout and we need a lot of space."

"Plus the kids associate their class areas—you were sweet to call
them rooms, dear—with age levels. My kids look forward to moving into the rear of the sanctuary as a sign of growing up," contrib-

uted Phyllis, a veteran of decades in the Sunday School. "Just ask your husband."

"No matter what we do, one class ends up in the kitchen and another in the entryway," added Bob. "There's no way around it. I gave this a lot of thought when I first found out I'd be teaching where each late-comer lets in the cold air when he or she opens the door to come in. But, over the years, I've kind of gotten used to it. And frequently I've turned it to advantage. Snow melting off boots and umbrellas set to dry make good illustrations, you know." Bob, thought Suzie, would never even consider that a half full cup was half empty, too, and in one sense that made her respect him all the more.

"What else you got for us tonight, Suzie. No sense spending any more time on what we can't improve on, anyhow."

"Sunday School classes in same room as last year," wrote Suzie in her notebook. She had long stopped wondering why no one else took notes and lately she had begun wondering why she did.

Custom, Consecration and Crisis

As Suzie was slowly learning, in an imperfect world that is fixed, it is a waste of time to attempt to reconsider the bases of present behavior. They already represent the best possible solution if only because they are the familiar and comfortable solution. Sometimes, though, this truth proceeds to a deeper level. The way we do things becomes the right, the morally right, way to do things. Whether our way of doing things is logical, rational, appropriate, efficient or even possible (some day I'd like to write on the miracle of the non-disappearance of the small church!) is not the question because the way in which we do certain things becomes part of the fixed order of the universe. To change these things is not a movement toward greater efficiency or reasonableness, no matter how much the pastor says it is. To change what is sacred is a movement toward disruption, disorientation and confusion. If Suzie had pushed to reassign Sunday School classrooms, the teachers might have lived with it (grumbling all the way). But when the pastor proposes that we move the Sunday morning worship service from 11 to 8 AM because half the people in town have only Sunday as a family day (implication—we don't want church to interrupt the family) and that no one milks cows any more (the supposed reason for the precedence of the 11 o'clock worship hour), small church people don't respond by counting cows and kids to see if the pastor is right. They respond first by panicking about the spiritual commitment of the pastor. ("He's not really saying that he wants more continuous hours of leisure, is he? If he is only that committed, how can he challenge us?") Or they respond by questioning the moral legitimacy of this group, "family" so-called. ("The church is family, too, Pastor.") Why should we who have sacrificed lo these many years for our Lord change our time of worship to accommodate those whose commitment to follow Christ is that low?

Eleven AM on Sunday morning is not a functionally derived time. It may have been once, but now it has become a sacred hour. Tampering with it is tantamount to tampering with the Ten Commandments. To either attempt we respond with moral shock, confusion, and, if persistent, outrage. So, too, the elements of worship, the frequency and manner of communion, the maintenance and use of the church building, the use of benevolences—some of our ways of doing go beyond tradition to sacredness. No attempt on our part to change them can go by unchallenged. One of my parishioners says, "If I am unable to worship on Sunday, the day isn't the same. In fact, the whole week seems confused." Worship is for her a point of orientation. A landmark in the flow of time. Being in God's house, in God's presence, is a sure and certain thing. It gives clarity and firmness to our time, our efforts, even our very selves. Whether all of what is sacred to us is sacred to God is open to question. But that it is sacred to us is fundamental. The way of organizing life with which we have become familiar orients our soul. Any change in these things threatens what we hold most dear—our very selves. (Jesus presupposes that we have heart, mind and soul so that we can give them to God in love.)

Any change attempt from the inside is seen as perverse, iconoclastic and disloyal. ("We thought you were one of us, Pastor.") Change from the outside, while just as threatening, can be dealt with more readily. For though it threatens, it is not the debilitation of self-threatening behavior. Rather, external threat motivates a survival response. It energizes the small church to put aside quarrels, to lock step, and beat back the challenge. That the small church mentality can cope better with external than internal threat leads readily to an understanding of certain phenomena. If, for example, the pastor is seen as the source of threat he or she will be moved to the outside, treated as a foreigner, made to feel the monolithic side of the congregation. For in this external position his or her threat can be better handled. If the threat is not personal but due to circumstance—for example, the church roof blows off in a storm—this threat to the valued order of things will, sometimes almost spontaneously, produce a response of congregational and community resources completely out of proportion to the everyday budget of the church. The initial response is, of course, to restore the past, to get things back to the way they were, the way they were when life felt right. So the roof is repaired and prayer proffered. But should this fail, the crisis reaches a dangerous yet potentially beneficial point. Dangerous because if no resolution occurs, disintegration, debilitating grief and death may very well result. (The roof stays unfixed and all of the accouterments of worshipping God suffer damage.) Yet potentially beneficial because it offers a deeper spiritual reality. The God behind our sacred cows becomes more clearly seen. His calling for a new day may be found. (We convene in the few dry pews to seek God's will and help—now new options become a Godsend!)

The moral for the pastor is simple. If you would bring change regarding that which is considered sacred by your small church people, make sure you locate the origin of the disruptive behavior in the external hand of God. Do not become a prophet crying in the wilderness, for that is surely where you will end up!

Habit

Small church people (all folk society people, actually) do not like to waste time reinventing the wheel. So most of what is done, or at least the way in which it is done, is done out of habit. Small Church behavior is habitual. It is done on the basis of experience, more than thought. A physiologist might say that the locus of direction for our actions is the medulla not the cerebrum. For years, almost beyond counting, my church has run a fund-raising chicken barbecue every August. The barbecue pit, picnic tables, the serving stations are all set up in the rear yard of the church. A couple of hundred people who are already familiar with our church situation find their way to the back and enjoy a good meal. For about 10 years now I have tried to persuade the chairman that the pit and table should be set up in the front yard of the church abutting the busiest street in town where walkers-by will smell the chicken and drivers-by will see the goings on, and more will decide to participate. Our diners would double in number and so would our "take." Logical, rational, efficient, profitable—you bet. Have we done it—not yet! The procedures for cooking and serving chicken in the back yard are well established. The call to rethink all that is too much to handle! We are habitual people.

Habits are hard to establish. They are unlikely to arise out of conscious decision. Rather they seem somehow to occur spontaneously in the midst of the ongoing life of the congregation. No individual can be thanked or blamed. "It's just the way we do things around here." I wish you could meet Clayton. He is in his late seventies, but he comes to worship regularly (in fact, the only worship he's missed in years is when he's been in the hospital), and he keeps track—a number of times he's gone over 100 continuous Sundays without missing a service! Now Clayton hands out the bulletins. How he ended up with that particular ministry is lost in the mists of time, but he is regular, dependable and faithful at it. A couple years back, the Deacons decided that the bulletins should be handed out by the ushers as they were seating people, a wise strategy for our busy summer Sundays. Clayton was asked to relinquish the bulletins. He wouldn't. So that Sunday two people handed out bulletins—one whose job it was by rationally delegated authority, the other whose job it was by custom and habit. Visitors couldn't figure out why they needed two identical bulletins! But (and this reflects the mutuality and interwovenness of corporate habitual behavior) our parishioners preferred to get their bulletins from Clayton and share a word about the Red Sox or activity down at the dock. The next Sunday habit won out and Clayton was restored to his rightful place as the one and only bulletin passer-outer.

Creating a new habit (e.g., ushers being responsible for the bulletins) is virtually impossible. This fact has undoubtedly caused more frustration to more small church pastors than any other small church dynamic. Yet there is a good side to it, believe it or not. The first benefit to note is that habits are a solution of sorts. Clayton is actually a very good bulletin minister. He comes early; doesn't miss anyone; greets everyone with a smile and many with cheery small talk; and he is there every Sunday. The slowness of his method and his "country" style are, on second thought, trivial prices to pay for such a faithful minister. The second benefit to keep in mind is this: as hard as habits are to establish, they are even harder to break! A good habit once in place in a small church can yield decades of benefits—a situation not likely to occur in mid- and large-sized churches and rationally structured organizations which do not live out of enacted memory.

Ten years ago a parishioner asked me if we could pray together on Saturday mornings and so our Men's Prayer Breakfast came into being—sort of. For months, despite repeated invitations to others, he and I were the only ones present. Finally, two others joined us. Then, one by one, men of the church—and the community—began attending. Now there are 8 to 12 men who meet every week. They will meet whether I come or not. They accept rotating host responsibilities; they call and pick each other up; they share and pray— and solve all the world's problems, whether I am there or not. (But, of course, I am there for I don't want to miss it either.) Frequently, they ignore my preparation and awkward spiritualizing; sometimes they seek my spiritual help; but usually the quality of sharing and caring, fellowship and support, is beyond anything I, alone, could offer. The Saturday morning Men's Prayer Breakfast is a decade old habit. It took a long time to establish it in the minds and hearts (and medulla) of our men. But now that it is there, nothing can stop it. And that's a good thing, for it is a habit that does a heavenly lot of good.

Good things such as the "Mary D" fund. Mary D., our State Nurse, had told one of our breakfasters that in her rounds she was saddened to note that a number of elderly people were not entitled to benefits because of being a few dollars over the annual income cap for the programs she happened to administer. When the Saturday Morning Group learned of the situation, $41 was spontaneously given and the idea of a fund administered in confidence by Mary D to help our needy neighbors had become a reality. By nightfall the man whose heart had been moved by Mary's plea and encouraged by the response of the men's breakfast cradled his phone. Now the fund stood at $1441! Over the last decade church offerings, concerts, anonymous donations, and CROP walks have helped to replenish the "Mary D" Fund. And Mary has distributed tens of thousands of dollars for fuel oil, food, electricity, medicines, etc., to our neighbors.

Good things such as advocacy at the Public Utilities Commission hearing. When the power company on our Island wanted to raise the rates (then the highest in the "continental U.S."), it was a big topic of conversation at our Saturday breakfast. Concern was expressed over the accounting set-up of the company and the impact the higher rates would have on the poor and those with fixed incomes. It was noted that the P.U.C. was holding a hearing that morning. We scattered from the breakfast, our feelings expressed, but with no plan of action. Concern welled up in my heart though, and I decided to attend the hearing. I watched amazed as one by one the men of the breakfast joined me in the hearing room! We spoke our piece and, if memory serves me, we were the only members of the public present. Did that one hearing result in the changed attitude of the P.U.C. toward granting rate increases? I doubt it, but it played a part, small but vital, in the overall movement.

Good things such as Operation Outreach, our church building renovation drive. How often was our drive chairman frustrated and weary over the five-year period of the drive? As he periodically shared his concern with the other men, encouragement, direction, energy, elbow grease, and even money poured forth in response. Today our drive is complete, our building refurbished and up to building code. To the men at the breakfast goes a lot of thanks.

The Men's Prayer Breakfast is a decade old habit, but what's wrong with a good habit?

Problem Solving in the Small Church

Problems confront every group of people. The small church is no exception. It is the manner in which problems are recognized and responded to that characterizes the small church.

In all groups, problems are recognized as dissonance—a discrepancy between the way things are and the way they ought to be. In a rationally structured organization, problems (discrepancies) occur when the present state of things differs significantly from the goals of the organization. If the rate of return of stock holdings in corporation Z is half that of a savings account at a local bank and one quarter of the return management predicted, a problem exists. If the new 22-room Christian Education wing was scheduled to be paid off in five years, but pledges actually coming in indicate a 20 year pay off schedule, a problem exists.

In a socially structured organization (a small church, for example), problems are registered as dissonance also, but not dissonance with the goals of the organization, for this organization has no goals. (This is not entirely true. Its goals, though frequently below the level of awareness, can be considered to be continuity over time [survival], congruity of behavior [maintaining the status quo], and recapturing the Garden of Eden [return to the good old days].) Rather, dissonance is registered when it occurs between the present state of things and how they used to be (when they were right). Problem registration, then, is not objective, nor is it subject to quantitative indices (except in very broad terms). It is a subjective sense, a feeling that things aren't right, a loss of congruency, a mismatch between experience and memory.

> Pastor, those Sunday School attendance comparisons you were sharing with us last month didn't register at all with me. But when I went to take my turn in the nursery Sunday and there wasn't one child for me to watch, it hit me. Why, I remember when it took three of us just to change the diapers and keep the bottles filled! That's the way it should be, pastor. What can we do?

Problems once registered may be dealt with by ignoring them.

This is a not uncommon small church response and sometimes a viable one! During my first year as pastor in my present parish, the Trustees virtually went broke to have our old, oversized building repainted. Alarms went off in my brain. We must prepare for this in the future, I pleaded, for we know that paint only lasts four or five years. Let us be good stewards and plan ahead and budget 25% each year of the last painting bill against the next one which will come as certainly as the sun rises and sets. I was eloquent in my efforts to protect my flock from the twin dangers of bankruptcy and unpaintedness. The Trustees were not visibly moved, but in order to get onto the next item of the agenda, voted to allocate a certain amount each year for painting, "as the pastor said." I breathed a sigh of relief. In my first year here, I had saved the church. I didn't expect a medal, but I did expect to get the money set aside. I got neither. Each year more pressing bills came up and the painting reserve was spent. I saw the sword of Damocles growing larger over our heads month by month. The paint began to blister, peel, crack and chalk before my very eyes. Meanwhile, though, a young man had moved into town and joined our church. He was an "independent contractor," which meant he enjoyed working on his own schedule doing odd jobs. The Trustees asked him if he painted. "Sure do." What would he charge to do the church? He gave a number slightly over minimum wage. "When can you start?" the Trustees asked in one voice. Miraculously reaching windows six feet beyond his fully extended ladder, he finished the job for a fraction of its previous cost. "Not to worry, pastor. The Lord will provide. He always has. I've seen it plenty of times before. When you don't know what to do, let it go. Something will come up. Just you wait and see."

It may be the problem solving procedure of an ostrich. Or it may be the way Christ's faithful down through the centuries have solved their problems. And when you think of it, what is budgeting compared to believing? Yet this is not faith abstracted and unrealistic. "I've seen it plenty of times before." It is a faith born of experience. Somehow the Lord has provided. Maybe it is this sense of the unpredictable happening when most needed that gets all folk people through. When the wilderness got too barren, manna and quail appeared. When the drought looked as though it would swallow every living thing, the heavens opened and a rich harvest was brought in. When my parish's island forbearers had farmed and fished to the limit of their ability and still found themselves short, somehow or other a storm-driven ship laden with lumber, coal, foodstuffs or cloth would crash onto their rock shores, and so provide for their needs. Unthinkable to plan for it, nevertheless, when it came hearts were raised Godward in gratitude. "No sense troubling yourself, pastor. God will provide."

But sometimes problems are not ignored. Rather, specific attempts are made to deal with them. The types of behavior exhibited in problem solving efforts can be divided into two general categories. These two categories reflect two different ways of thinking, of understanding life, of operating in a social world. The first category we may call analytical, scientific, rational, functional or organizational. The second we may call holistic, creative, intuitive, expressive or social. The specific name we choose to use is much less important than the realization that the former approach is the one taught and valued in our dominant culture, and the latter is the one which is usually operational in the small church.

The first problem solving approach is cognitive, objective and predicated on increased understanding. It is based on certain assumptions. One is that behavior proceeds from intention. (Those who are not enamored of this position would claim that this proposition is so patently untrue that its opposite is common knowledge picturesquely expressed in a saying regarding the pavement on the road to hell.) A second assumption is that "life" can be stopped, that the problem area can be frozen and considered in its essence and at one's leisure. A third assumption is that the relevant variables and facts are accessible and comprehensible. The potency of the scientific approach over the last few centuries has led many to use it unquestioningly. But small church people are seldom comfortable with this approach.

At any rate, a typical sequence of this approach is as follows:

1. The problem area is frozen and one specific problem is focused upon.

2. This problem is clearly defined (quantitatively, if possible).

3. The problem, its causes, implications and ramifications are analyzed. What forces have brought the problem into being, keep it in place, and resist actual or potential solution efforts?

Next, these steps are taken:

4. List solution states. Solutions must be specific, objective, recognizable and measurable.

5. Choose solution state to be achieved (with criteria used for selection).

6. Devise an action plan with goals, objectives and strategies including performance and time criteria.

7. Implement action plan.

8. The problem is solved after solution is effected, generalized and stabilized.

(Note: Above steps are taken from my notes from a seminary course on church administration.)

By way of illustration, we could go through these steps with a sample problem.

1. Within a seven-day period, three people complain to you, the Trustee Chair, about the low level of cleanliness of the sanctuary.

2. After an extensive interview with each of the three, you determine that the problem boils down to this:

a. The three have been seen to have dusty seats on their navy blue dresses while shaking hands with the pastor after worship. All three claim to have been clean upon entering the pews.

b. Dust in the pipes, it is alleged, has accumulated to the point that it is the cause of the asthmatic hum in the organ.

c. Dust on the communion table is so thick that the pastor not only could but did write in it with his finger, "What hath God rot?" (This message was deemed by the three almost as bad a problem as the dust, but it is beyond the parameters of this problem specification.)

3. You decide this problem, its causes and (potential) cures, need further analysis, so you administer a questionnaire to the congregation following worship the next Sunday. The computer-tabulated results indicate that 31 out of 32 adults present and voting (all did vote as only then did you permit them to leave the sanctuary after the benediction) felt the sanctuary could be cleaner. (Incidentally, the one vote, a write-in, "the sanctuary is perfectly clean and has been for years," came from Mildred who for the last 10 years has received $4 per week to clean the church building in its entirety. She has quit her cleaning position over the "questionnaire outrage" and is threatening to quit the church. The pastor wants to know why you couldn't have bought her a new dust rag and given her a bit of encouragement instead of "making a big stink.")

4. You determine that the solution states are as follows:

a. No cleaning. When church gets filthy someone will notice and spontaneously and graciously clean up.

b. Apologize to Mildred.

c. Raise the cleaning budget to $30 a week and hire a Felix Unger type. (Take the additional $26 out of the pastor's salary.)

5. You select solution 4b. "Apologize to Mildred." After all, she is your wife.

6. Action Plan: Today speak to Mildred. Tomorrow buy new dust mitt. Next day Mildred resumes cleaning.

7. As above, except that the store was out of dust mitts ("has been for twelve years"), so an old hanky was substituted.

8. Problem Solved. Solution monitored by ongoing observation of all navy blue seats in line after worship.

The second "problem-solving" approach diverges widely from the analytical approach and is predicated upon a different mindset. Its operating assumptions are antithetical to those in the first problem solving approach. This approach is intuitive, subjective and is not necessarily dependent on rational comprehension. It is based on the assumption that much more than intention is necessary for behavioral change. One of my deacons struggled with her smoking habit. Finally, she resolved to quit. Eventually she did. "How did you do it," I asked her. "I didn't do it at all," she answered, "God did." "Well, how did God quit?" I wondered. "I knew I needed to quit. I knew that no matter how much I intended to quit, I couldn't. So I started praying for God to remove all desire to smoke from me. It took six months, but He did it. I didn't have to force myself at all." In the realm of habitual behavior there is no direct connection between intention and behavioral change. Intention is not irrelevant. For my deacon it provided the occasion for the Holy Spirit's work. But it does not lead directly to behavioral change. (This is a good place to note the object of behavioral change. In the rationally structured organization, intentionality leads to behaviors that accomplish a programmatic goal. In the socially structured organization, behavioral changes are directed at "our way of life." Therefore, they are both much more difficult to achieve and much more long lived, if achieved.)

The second assumption of the analytical approach is that life can be stopped and analyzed. In the intuitive approach life is not stoppable. It goes merrily along. It is organic, ongoing, alive. Understandings and actions are accomplished on the run. It is harder to hit a moving target, but small church people would say those are the only targets there are. The third (and related) assumption of the analytical model, that the problem-causing elements are distinct from the problem-solving, is patently untrue in the small church. Pogo's aphorism, "We have met the enemy and he is us," is closer to being true. At least when we meet the problem in the small church we realize how "married" to it we are!

If we were to analyze this intuitive, or creative approach, it would flow along these lines:

1. Dissonance arises. The individual or the group becomes

aware of a conflict between what is actually occurring and what one (or all) is used to having occur. This dissonance is intuitive and generalized. It is a gut feeling and is only focused to an "area" and not to a quantitatively specified problem statement.

2. The problem is "cooked." The small church problem solver realizes that all behaviors are interconnected, life is of a piece, and that any change in the established patterns of behavior will be tough to accomplish. Therefore, there is no desire to "rush into things." There is no highly specific goal state, for the full implications of new integrated patterns of behavior are usually beyond specification if not comprehension. Rather a general feel of how things "ought to be" emerges in the problem solver. Frequently, this is little more than a desire to return to the way things were before the discrepancy was noted. But how to do so is never clear. So the problem is cooked. It is put on the back burner to let simmer. This can be done verbally. If so, the resulting behavior is indistinguishable from "gossip." But it can also be done neurally. If so, it resembles a scanning process, usually unconscious to the one or ones engaged in it. The past is sifted. Sensitivity to "clues" in the present is heightened. Behavioral clones are toyed with. (These are actions that look and feel like "the way we do things" but which differ slightly in the direction of a solution.) Heretofore overlooked connections are made. "Cooking" may seem a peculiar way to solve a problem, but, I believe, it is in fact the way in which most problems get viably solved. A rational frontal attack on a problem seldom allows all the solution elements which are possible in a more intuitive, subjective, and/or subconscious approach to emerge. I'll 'fess up. "Cooking" is how I solve the weekly "problem" of my sermon. Early in the week I determine the Biblical and thematic direction for the sermon. Then I just let it cook until Saturday. Consciously and unconsciously I "live" this truth all week. Seldom has the Lord disappointed me in making it more vivid and profound to my soul. (How seldom my parishioners are disappointed is another question!) It is not just that the sermon problem is solved "on the run." It is also that "the run" is the solution!

3. Then "Aha!" occurs. At some point in the cooking process, if a solution is to emerge, a new connection is made. The problem is seen in a new light which illumines the direction for a solution. The connection of a disparate element is sensed. A way to get something done that fits like an old shoe emerges. "Of course" is the typical response. The solution was staring me in the face; it was on the tip of my tongue; it was as plain as the nose on my face; I almost missed the forest for the trees. All of a sudden the solution clicks into place. "Aha!"

A dramatic example is seen in the conversion of the Apostle Paul. His struggle against Christianity frequently "boiled over" into violence against the followers of the Prince of Peace. The spiritual wrestling that had consumed his life for months ended in one brilliant moment of clarity when he realized that Jesus was Lord and all he had been doing was railing against reality! In that instant it all fell into place. The problem of spiritual acceptance was granted (not through his efforts, but) in Christ's grace. And Paul's life also demonstrates the two further points of the creative problem solving process; one, that "aha!" leads to evangelism and, two, that the conviction of this new found truth is beyond the need for proof in the social world.

4. Aha! to Evangelism. When the connection is made in this manner the solution cannot be contained. If the solution is a sermon, it has to be preached. If a work of art, it has to be painted or sculpted. If an insight, it has to be written or spoken. If a ministry, it has to be enacted. It is not complete until it works itself out in expression and actuality. It is not a private solution. It is a gift to the body! Others must be told.

5. Conviction. The truth of this solution is given in the Aha! It is not necessary, nor even subject to, testing in the social world. Just as with the Apostle Paul, my faith in Jesus Christ is not dependent upon any particular event in my experience. (If bad things happen to me, I do not feel that God was an illusion, unable to protect me from evil. Rather, I ask for strength to survive and grow; I ask what good may come of this, what am I to learn because of this. Everything that happens to me is tested by my faith in Jesus. My faith is not tested by what happens to me.) The solution is prior to subsequent experience. The former conditions the latter. (This may in part explain why it is frequently so frustrating to a rationally structured person to argue with one with a small church outlook. Logic and reason carry little weight. Conviction born of experience is all.)

Again, let us see how these steps work out in regard to the dirty church problem.

1. Dissonance arises. Within a seven-day period, three people complain to you, the Trustee Chair, about the low level of cleanliness of the sanctuary. You think about the comments and recall that when you lit the candles last Sunday the communion table was dusty, the organ does sound a bit rheumy, and half of the chandelier bulbs are burned out. You remember when, as a boy, you had to take your boots off on the top step to keep from trudging any dirt into the perfectly clean sanctuary. You remember cleanliness

was an obsessive idea—the concept of an immaculately clean church, spotless before the throne of God. You remember what a shock it was when you found out that "the immaculate conception" meant something entirely different to Catholics.

2. The problem is cooked. That the complaints of uncleanliness are justified is unfortunate. It would have been so much easier to say, "Well, we'll see what can be done," in lieu of doing anything. But they are right. It is dirty. But it is also unfair to blame Mildred. She's had to take a full time job. She has all she can do to cook for you and the kids and clean your house. The church just gets a once over lightly. And, after all, she only gets $4 a week—unchanged in years. And she only took it on ten years ago when Rev. Parsons asked her to on account of the "immaculate" ladies had finally succumbed to their cleanliness and now were next to Godliness. He was going to organize a group of families to clean on a rotating weekly basis. Another one of his good ideas that we never quite got around to doing. Too bad. It was simple and could be fun and would save $4 a week. (Of course, Mildred gives it back anyhow so it wouldn't mean any more money into the plate, but it would look like less out, anyhow! And wasn't Mildred just talking to you last week about turning it over to someone if she could only figure out who?) Well, now, that rotating idea isn't bad. We usher a family at a time and it works out to only once a quarter.

3. Aha! What if each ushering family came in an hour early— they usually do, anyhow—and vacuumed and dusted—it would be like our service to God. We would each have a part in keeping God's house A-1. then instead of complaining, we could put our energy to good use. What an idea!

4. Evangelism. You decide to call an emergency meeting of the Trustees an hour before church this Sunday. We'll go over the whole idea and work any bugs out.

5. Conviction. Now people will be proud to usher folks into the pews they've just polished!

Summary

Problems in the Small Church are registered and solved differently. They are registered as deviations from the ideal past. Problems are felt and solutions are mulled. Particular behaviors are less a part of a viable solution than is forming new habits, finding integrated patterns of behavior which fit and feel right. Rationality and intentionality have only a subordinate role to play. People, their relations and behaviors, their interests and egos, their histories and turf constitute both the building blocks of a solution and the obstacles to a solution. That is what makes problem-solving in the small church so interesting and exhausting!

What Motivates Behavior in the Small Church

Asking "Why?" constitutes an interesting window on how people think. Not only the content but the form of the answer reveals the structures of significance in one's mental world.

My youngest child has just passed the "Why?" stage. Everything he observed, every statement of mine was greeted with the single syllable "Why?" Foolishly, thinking this to be a question of substance, I would answer him, as simply as possible. No matter how obvious the content of my response, it was invariably greeted with another "Why?" This continued until my patience wore thin, whereupon the interchange reached its finale with an exasperated "Because!" This was great fun for little Jason and I suppose (now that he is into the "No" stage, I have enough distance on the Why? stage to ask "Why?" myself!) that it was fun for two reasons. The first was that his little mind was starting to grasp the connectedness of life. Things can exist not only in physical connection, but also in logical, sequential and causal relationship. It must be exciting for him to begin the process of working that through. There is also, I believe, a second reason for this behavior and that is that it connects him to me. the whole interchange became a game in which his relationship to me is explored and tested. "Why?" is a way of charting his world.

"Why?" asked of an upper level manager or bureaucrat is answered in terms of goals. Whatever the behavior of the organization—stock offerings, public questionnaires, new advertising campaign, expanding product research and development, unveiling a new corporate logo, making a political contribution—all are explainable in terms of means toward a specified end. (Even if actions are taken because "that's the way we do things around here," this would never be articulated to a superior or the public at large. Habit is not an acceptable reason for behavior. Some rationale would be expressed to defend questioned behavior in terms of goal attainment.) Why? becomes a rational exercise in causality. Mission statements, goals, objectives and strategies are all connected to each other by "why" (going one direction on the flow chart) and "how" (going the other). Why? reveals the logic behind a rationally structured organization.

Ask a small church person Why? though, and an entirely different response will ensue. The first and most likely response will be confusion. Not only is the question difficult to answer, the reason for asking it is almost beyond comprehension. Small church society is not primarily self-reflective. Self-analysis, asking why about their behavior is not an ordinary activity. The answer is so obvious as to remove the need for the question. The behavior is its own rationale. We do *this* because *we* do this. What we do and how we do it are almost never at issue because we do what we always have done, and we do it as we always have done it. To ask why is almost to question the integrity of the group, to shake the foundations that hold us up. We may have forgotten why we started to behave this way, but now we do it because it's our way of doing things, our way of enacting and living out life. So the first response to why? is confusion and, if pushed, defensiveness.

But if the why? question is answered (and it seems to me that it is more frequently answered in the small church when not asked) it takes a peculiar form. It is not the indefinite chain of the child feeling out connections in life. Nor is it the crisp logic of the organizational man. Rather, the answer to Why? in the small church takes the form of a story, usually about a spiritual forbearer. Our parish celebrates a peculiar institution called Roll Call. I had never even heard of this practice before assuming the pastorate here (but since, I have learned that it was a popular custom decades back and is still practiced by a few churches here and there). What was it? I needed to know. Well, I soon learned. On Roll Call Sunday, mysteriously the Sunday closest to October 23, the entire membership list was called out during worship. Fewer than one in four was present to respond. Why did we recite names of people long uninterested in the parish, of people who moved to California decades ago, of people whom we later learned were dead for years? I couldn't figure it out. Of those who answered, three of four simply said, "Here" or some version thereof. The more articulate announced "Present," the more folksy, "Uhuh" or "Ayya," and a couple who were hard of hearing said nothing, but the stage whispers of their pew mates indicated their presence to all. Although why any of these responses were necessary was unclear to me since any darn fool could tell who was here and who wasn't. However, the final quarter of a quarter shared a scripture verse or a brief thought. Ah, I reasoned, we wade through it all to get these nuggets of truth. It kind of redeemed the situation. (Until the next year when I heard the same verses from the same people, as if it was their theme verse, learned in Sunday School or given at baptism, and designating them forever, like a second name.) Why, I still wondered. Then two days later the church erupted in a bustle of activity. Cooked turkeys showed up. Carvers, table setters, squash peelers all were working as if choreographed. Within hours a couple of hundred people were seated, fed, and things cleaned up. I was impressed, but still mystified. Then I noticed that our treasurer sat at a small table by the front door and collected donations from everyone entering. These she duly recorded on a lined, yellow sheet of paper. (She was a school teacher.) As the clean-up crew finished , she whispered to me. "It looks good. We did real well tonight." "Oh, great," I whispered back, carefully guarding our little secret. Later I received a letter from a shut-in member expressing her sorrow at not being present for Roll Call *to renew her faith in Jesus Christ*. Was that what was going on? Or were we simply trying to balance the budget, using turkey instead of tithing? My Why?s going unheeded, I finally stumbled on the combination. I asked our treasurer, "When did we start observing Roll Call?"

> Oh, that was back in 1900 when Dr. Roberts was pastor. The furnace broke down and he wanted to raise $300 to fix it before winter set in. Since the church was founded on October 23, 1765, he selected the Sunday closest to that date, called it Roll Call, said he was going to call the Membership Roll, and asked the church members to renew their commitment to Christ and His church by saying and giving. He got his money and we've been doing it ever since.

Why? Why do we call the Roll eighty-eight years later? Because we need spiritual recommitment? Undoubtedly we do, but that doesn't explain it. Because we need the money? Undoubtedly, but that is only part of it. We do it because we've done it. We do it now because Dr. Roberts started it then. We call the roll because that is what *we* do. Whether it is logical or illogical, appropriate or not, helpful or not more or less misses the point. We do it because we do it. Because Dr. Roberts was our pastor and we continue to be his people.

The Personal World of Small Church Experience

The small church world is above all a personal world. "A 'person' may be defined as that social object which I feel to respond to situations as I do, with all the sentiments and interests which I feel to be my own; a person is myself in another form, his qualities and values are inherent within him, and his significance for me is not merely one of utility. A 'thing,' on the other hand, is a social object which has no claim upon my sympathies, which responds to me, as

I conceive it, mechanically; its value for me exists in so far as it serves my end. In the folk society all human beings admitted to the society are treated as persons; one does not deal impersonally ('thing-fashion') with any other participant in the little world of that society."[1]

Like a folk society, the significant reality in small church society, the reality that motivates behavior and organizes life, as profit is to business and knowledge is to science, is not things or ideas. It is not even people per se. It is the relationships between people. Of course, individual people are necessary if interpersonal relations are to occur, but individualism is not the significant reality of the small church. How we are connected and placed in a personal world, the movements within our social world, how we are rooted and placed among whom we think of as "us," this is the focus of small church concern. This is the small church world.

This world, personal and relational by nature, is really "out there." But it is also "in here." It is inside the perception, mind and heart of small church people. What small church people really want is to live together, to receive the enjoyment that comes from being a part of this particular social arrangement. Now, of course, in order to live together, one must also live. And so, building a home, tending a garden, working a job are also part of life, and a very important part. But the people in one's life are not seen as instruments toward the end of accomplishing these goals, as much as those activities are seen as necessary to maintain our life together.

One could speak about the goal of life in mainstream American culture as the imprinting of one's ego on one's environment. Thus millions are motivated to build up their world (their business, their career, their bank accounts, their net worth) as a testament to their superiority. It is not enough to be financially successful. One's self-worth must be demonstrably confirmed by relative material success. Other people then become instruments of one's self interest (e.g., employees, business and political contacts, technical resource providers) or the background against which one's achievements are made obvious. Their world then is seen as the material which they can organize toward their goal which must yet be achieved and people are understood as instruments of this quest. The "essential" small church position is in logical antithesis to this extreme statement of the mainstream position. The small church person's world looks different. His/her main goal is not to be achieved: it is a given—the pre-existent world of social roles, relationships and intercourse of which they are a part by nature. Although in reality the behavior of small church people over time will maintain, modify or erode that social world; nevertheless, it is perceived as something

essentially beyond their power to transform. And persons and relationships are seldom perceived as functional toward the achieve-
ment of a separate goal, but rather as what life is all about in the
final analysis.

The tensions in my own heart and mind may illustrate this
point. Over the past five years, my wife has been successful in a
small business she runs in our town. So we have gone from hardly
having two nickels to rub together to being people upon whom in-
surance agents deem it worthwhile to call. We have indulged ourselves in such luxuries as paving our driveway, taking a vacation to
Barbados, and buying an investment property. We have gone from
two young kids with stars in their eyes and water behind their ears
to people with investment decisions to make and taxes to pay. We
have arrived. We are successful. And we are conflicted. Not morally,
for honesty and stewardship have characterized both the income
and the outgo of the monies. Not morally, but socially. Our neighbors make cracks about our driveway. "Looks like the suburbs,"
they say. We are cut to the quick. "Where are you going this year?"
they wonder. So defensive have I gotten that I have come up with
excuses to justify the demonstrations of our success (Barbados—it
was the cheapest vacation package we could find; the driveway—for
what we were paying each year in grading, we just decided to do it
right once and for all; the property—it was sold to someone else
but when the deal fell through, we just stumbled on to it). Our
year-round people are the fourth poorest in the state. For eight
years we were one with them in economic marginality. Now, our
very success has strained our social world. We feel embarrassed to
have achieved a modest measure of material surplus. We feel awkward when we once felt completely at home. One of our church
members solved this problem. One day he won the state lottery.
With his winnings he threw a chicken barbecue for the whole island. With the monies left after that he started a scholarship fund.
Needless to say he is still very central in the life and heart of the
community.

That success should be antithetical to one's social world is only
a problem to people who perceive the world personally. Small
church people understand the world as ultimately composed of persons and their relationships. And we see the world as ultimately
personal, too. Since what we value is the personal, we see the personal in all that we value. Everything reminds us of persons. "Which
way is she blowing today?" you will overhear the fishermen ask regarding the wind as they decide whether to take their boats out,
boats to which they always refer as "she" or "her," never "it."

The Trustees had organized their annual foray into the bowels of the church, otherwise known as "Clean Up Day." I grabbed hold of a board hidden in the darkest corner and pulled it out under the dangling light bulb to get a good look see. It was dusty and moldy with faded and chipped paint, but "First Baptist Church" could just be discerned. Just as I was about to suggest chopping it up for firewood, one of the ladies present remarked, "Oh, look. That's the sign my grandfather painted. There's his initials. This hung over the front door for many a year. Here, let me set it down in a safe place." And she took it from me. An old sign? Firewood? Nope. That was her grandfather almost as much as if it had been his bones. That old piece of wood reminded her of him, his role in the church, the church as it had been, her childhood and her life in the church. It was precious. And it continues to survive every clean up day. (Now *I* protect it!) Things are not just things. They are connections to loved ones. They are symbols of our social world. They are evidences of persons left in physical form to remind us of who we are as persons—their descendants, the ones to whom they have passed the torch.

The world view of small church people is built of people and relationships, and even impersonal things are "personalized" when viewed from this perspective. That is the mental world of small church people. But how do they move in this world? What is their thought and logic? To the uninitiated (e.g., suburban raised, seminary trained, rational pragmatists), small church thinking is patently illogical. It yields no satisfactory sense. But this is to look at it from an external perspective. When viewed internally, it is consistent and even has its own logic. I like to think of the small church approach as being more psycho-logical than logical. In other words, the question in the small church is never, as it is in business, what is the most efficient means of accomplishing the goal that management has selected. Using a logical approach, a business firm would marshal cash and financing, experts and skills, data and strategies. It would all be very rational and successful. But in the small church virtually all of these tools are non-existent. Extra cash is hard to come by; financing is often taboo; there are no experts; skills are well-hidden; there is no data except feeling; and strategies are simply what we are used to doing. The only thing left to the small church is people. So the question in the small church is never simply one of logic. It is always psycho-logical (internally) and sociological (externally). Who really wants to do this? And how can others be motivated to help or not hinder?

Through ten years of experience, sometimes thrilling, sometimes bitter, I have come to know pretty well who in my parish have taken upon themselves the ministry of inertia. "If God wanted us to fly, he'd have given us wings." (Actually, this ministry can be positive if it weeds out the bad ideas before they become habits.) And I have come to know who have taken upon themselves the ministry of improvements. (Pastors, beware of these people, too. They can poop you out faster than the inertial people can frustrate you!) Some of our inertial people will exert enormous amounts of energy in improving what we already do. But to do something new or different is beyond their support, if not their comprehension. Furthermore, I have also noted that some who will fight an "improvement" tooth and nail become proud as peacocks after the improvement has become our regular way of doing things. So things proceed in our small church world, not according to a "logical" progression, but like a river meandering through a valley, skirting rock outcroppings, looking for the "way of the possible."

Parameters of Small Church Mentality

The Different Understanding of Time

I have always had trouble managing time. My inability to organize my time is exceeded only by my terror at missing an obligation or a deadline. Thus do I get things done. If God wanted me to be on time, He'd have given me a wristwatch—which He did for my birthday! So, I decided, enough bungling around. It's time I got organized. I enrolled in a time management seminar which I attended, although late. The leader had twenty-one Tinker Toy things that locked into each other. He called these the building blocks of our week, morning, afternoon, and evening, the seven days. He said professional clergy persons should be spending 12 to 16 time blocks per week on ministry (that's two blocks each day, six to eight days a week). Piece of cake, I thought. Family time—three blocks a week should do it. A couple of blocks for personal time. And whatever is left for painting the house, balancing the checkbook and cleaning the basement. (I spend almost a block a week in the bathroom, but I couldn't see how to work this in.) I left the seminar that afternoon (having invested two time blocks) tired but inspired. Soon I would be organized.

I worked hard at my blocks. But apparently my emotional block and my parish block, not to mention my island block, were greater than my time blocks. I watched as people burst into my sermon preparation block to ask counsel regarding their marriage. I saw my sleeping block fade into consciousness as I stood by a parish family in the wee hours of the morning watching their home burn to the ground. I watched as my visitation block slipped away as, one after another, people stopped me outside the post office to confer regarding some issues they were facing. I despaired of getting anything done. People in this parish just don't work in blocks.

In fact, time for small church-small town people is not blockable. It is not "chronological" even. Sure, we have watches and calendars, but they are mostly used to tell us where we thought we were going to be when we actually are where we are. Something like the "You are here" spot on the floor maps at the museum. Time for us is not a uniform quantity like lumber which can be cut to fit. Time is simply the context within which the significant events of our lives occur. When it ain't blowing a gale and the cod are running, the fishermen are gone. When I go to visit Aunt Gladys, she can't imagine that I have three other people to see that afternoon. She thinks she is the only one. And I better think it, too. If worship runs overtime and, in a dither, I apologize to the deacons afterward, they look at me strangely. "Well, the sermon was good, the music was great, a lot of important things were said during sharing time. It didn't *feel* long. Don't worry about it, pastor." (Emphasis added) Time is what's happening, not what the clock ticked.

So is time experienced in the small church. But where is it leading? In our dominant American society time is linear. It is going somewhere. History and technology are moving. If you're not gaining ground, you're losing ground. Nothing stands still. Change is inevitable. Progress is what it is all about. "Every day, in every way, I am getting better." That history has a linear component is evident to small church people as well as the rest of society. Small church people know what year their church was founded, some of the circumstances at that time, ups and downs of their church over the years, which pastors succeeded whom, and what building improvements were made in what order. But small church people recognize another aspect of time—its cyclical nature. For small church people the course of history is not so much directional as it is repetitive. Just as the seasons follow each other in an ordered sequence, so, too, the seasons of the affairs of humankind follow each other in a dependable sequence. Boom follows bust; neither lean nor fat years are forever; fashions come and go and come round again; each succeeding generation makes the same mistakes its parents made. Nothing is new under the sun.

I brought a lot of energy to the early years of my pastorate here. I organized and helped start up new programs left and right. We began a Vacation Bible School, an ecumenical choir, a church fair, a Bible Study program, and on and on. As a young pastor, fresh out of seminary, I was proud of what we were doing. I was pleased

with the new directions our church was taking. Our new initiatives
were exciting and gratifying to me. And most people appreciated
the "new life" the church was experiencing. Most, but not all. One
particular individual had a standard and, to me, frustrating response
to every new idea I proposed. "So you want to do 'Y.' Well, that's
nothing new. Why when pastor 'X' was here we used to. . . ." (And
there followed a glowing account of a past program of the same
type but so much superior to what I had in mind.) In my own mind
I was the young, new and brilliant pastor proposing energetic, new
and brilliant programs to my flock. In her mind, young, new and
brilliant things did not exist. There is nothing new under the sun.
We simply add on variations to the themes of the past. By recalling
that past she was able to integrate and accept my ideas. What I
thought was her "Big Deal!" was really her way of saying "O.K. I've
seen that before and it's O.K.—we're still here, aren't we?" At that
level of my personal maturity, I was motivated by linear time (progress) and debilitated by repetitive time (that's been done before).
She was the opposite. Cyclical time freed her to accept the vicissi-
tude of the day. Lately I have come around more to her position.
Time (history, progress) is not a vector shot out into infinity. Rather,
it is a pendulum whose excesses are righted by its return swing. I
find hope and consolation in this perception, and so, I believe, do
most of my small church brothers and sisters.

So time is marked by happenings. Secondly, what's happening
has happened before. And, thirdly, the first time it happened was
the best. I put a lot of time and effort into sermons, committee
meetings and Bible studies trying to motivate my parish the way I
was motivated: to see God's kingdom come to earth, to look forward to God's new heaven and new earth, to look boldly into the
future which God was preparing for us. It excited me to envision a
better tomorrow and it energized me to work for it. But it didn't
seem to do much for my parishioners. Most of the folk seemed to
be enervated not energized by my aspirations. They got tired just
listening to my hopes for the future. I began to wonder what was
going on. First, I wondered what was wrong with them. In order to
find out, I decided I'd hush up a bit and listen to what they were
saying. And I heard things like, "Amy? She doesn't get out much any
more, and it hurts her not to be able to help out at Roll Call. I remember as a kid seeing her work in the church kitchen all day
long—morning 'til night—getting the food ready. But she can't
now, so I guess I'm one of the ones to pick up the slack." And
"When Dr. Roberts was here, the building was really cared for. If a
repair was needed, he'd go up and down Main Street till he'd raised
the money. Then the men of the church rolled up their sleeves and

did it." and "When Rev. Pratt was in the hospital after that hit and run accident, the deacons did the whole service. For weeks on end they preached, prayed, the whole thing, A to Z. So I don't see why we can't pinch hit when you're away, Pastor." And slowly it began to dawn on me that I was going about this all wrong. I was using the wrong image. It was the "Garden of Eden" not the "New Jerusalem" that inspired them. And I was heading in the wrong direction. It was the "Good Old Days" not a "Bright New Tomorrow" that motivated them. They were energized to restore the good of the past, but not to create a new future. Yesterday not tomorrow attracted their interest and concern.

This realization has made a profound difference in my ministry. I have become a history buff. The oral and written history of our church, I snatch up whenever I can. I structure ways in which our history can be explored, shared and re-experienced. As pastor, I feel free to add the "therefore so ought we to be." Whether we are yet is open to debate, but that people are listening is beyond question. And I am having fun rummaging around the attic of our church's memory discovering spiritual treasures. For small church people time goes the "wrong" way—away from what is new and better. It goes toward the good that was, or that was thought to be.

The Different Understanding of Space

Recently our head trustee and I went up to talk to the State Fire Marshal. Before he'd answer our questions, he had a few of his own. What is the square footage of your building? Neither of us knew. Well, how big is your sanctuary—what dimensions? Not sure, exactly, but in the summer 120 fit in without being crowded and in the winter 60 can spread out without getting lost. He wasn't sure that was very helpful. I thought it was great—met our needs exactly. How about Fellowship Hall? he wanted to know. That I know, I said. It is exactly one folding table set with a chair at each end wide and exactly six folding tables fully set long. And it was just big enough to have a Sunday School class at one end and the coffee hour hostess setting up at the other without disturbing each other. And the food cooperative that distributed from there had just the right amount of space as long as they did the pet food outside. And it was plenty big enough for the Scouts, our annual Christmas party, and our choir to get ready in. However, it was a bit small for our VBS closing program, refreshments following, and our Christmas Eve giving out of presents. That's nice, he said, but why don't you come back with measurements and a floor plan?

Once when a wedding ceremony took me to New York state I

indulged a long deferred desire and sneaked up to Cooperstown to visit the Baseball Hall of Fame. I wandered around and just soaked up the whole place—plaques on the wall with the faces and the stories of the greats of baseball. In my mind flashed instant replays of those I'd seen in action and imaginative recreations of those from before my time. The belated honor paid to the greats of the Negro leagues, the exploits of those whose names were lost in the mists of time, the contributions of those who made the game into today's national pastime. Truly, I felt a sense of awe.

Maybe nothing so dramatic occurs when I wander around my church. But I am never there alone. On the hymn board are the numbers hand done by Stan Pratt. The baptistry curtain, fresh and clean, reminds me of the struggle Barbara and I had to replace the tattered old one. The organ reminds me of the faithful and creative services of Carrie for almost two decades now. The walls painted a few years back by Wilbur, and the chandeliers recently cleaned by John who doesn't care for heights. There's where Clayton sits getting ready to hand out the bulletins. And each pew almost shaped to the posteriors of its occupants every Sunday for years and years. In Fellowship Hall is the "Flea Market" that Brad oversees and the table that Scouts "wounded." Eileen picked out the floor tiles—pretty but hard to keep clean—and David painted the walls because he got tired of looking at the plaster chips. In the foyer hangs a picture of Nathan Mott who built the building a century ago. Only our oldest members remember him. Steve, who's Jewish but worships with us occasionally, sent his painting crew down to give the walls their fresh look. And there's the light fixture which Charlie fought so long and hard in the Trustee Board to get replaced. It remains as a monument to his (our) failure and the nature of the small church! If you look hard at the inside of the front door you will see certain scratches imperfectly concealed by compound and paint incurred on the day I forgot my dog inside and went merrily along home. Speaking of dogs, you will note beneath the fourth pew near the wall in the sanctuary a small rug. That's for Ina, Duffy's seeing eye dog. He comes to church regularly and yawns (three times last Sunday) during my sermons. Bea Dodge used to bring her dog to worship, too. If he didn't care for my sermons, he just fell asleep at her feet. She died not too long after he did. And. . . .

The church building, you see, is more than a physical space to gather in. It is a Hall of Memories. It brings to mind those who have been important to us, to Christ's church and God's work in this place. It is sacred not only because it is the house of God, but also because it houses the memory of those who are significant to us, who kept and keep the church going, who have given shape not only to the church building, but also to our lives, who have been for us the incarnation of God's love and care. So space in the small church can never be dealt with only quantitatively. It also has a personal and therefore a sacred dimension.

The Purpose of Behaviors in a World That Doesn't Change

I am a convert to the small church view of the world. I was raised to view the world abstractly, analytically and objectively. Gradually has my mind been transformed to utilize and value a folk mentality. However, sometimes my unregenerate world view seeps through. One such occasion occurred after the acquisition by our church of a word processor. It was the gift of a church member to facilitate the publication of a small church and our own parish newsletters. I was thrilled with my new toy. I experimented with it, worked the bugs out, and utilized it to "go to press" more quickly and easily than before. And (foolishly) I wrote an article in our parish newsletter explaining that we were now "on line," that only one in one hundred churches in our land has a computer, and that, therefore, we were on the cutting edge of ministry, in the vanguard of tomorrow. Superlatives flowed like water, for I was proud of our little church. The parishioners, however, weren't so sure. It struck them the other way. "If ninety-nine out of every one hundred churches get by fine without one of those fancy machines, why do we need it, Pastor?" I should have realized. I am a pastor; I write and speak to various groups; I edit a small church newsletter—all because it is important to me to change the world for the better. But I have to constantly remind myself that at this point I differ from my small church people. They do not desire to be in the vanguard of anything. Progress is understood as perfection—working the bugs out of our present ways of doing things. It is not important to them to leave their impression on the world. For they have already "impressed" the world that is vital to them, the social world in which they live and move and have their being. What they really want to do is live out the existing patterns of life and enjoy them to the full. Their goal, simply put, is maintenance not transformation. Their motivation is to preserve—preserve the existing patterns of behavior, preserve the existing rhythms of life, preserve the feeling of all being right in their world. (Not that all is right. There are plenty of wrongs in their world—as the delight in gossip attests—but these are the right wrongs, typical, human foibles. Evil wrongs are those things which disrupt the integration of their thought-action world.)

That behavior is more directed at preservation than transformation in the small church world is reinforced by a further perception of reality. That is that the environment is essentially fixed and un-changeable. One's personal life and, maybe, one's family life may be subject to transformation by personal initiative, but one's potency decreases rapidly as one moves beyond the self. The physical, politi-cal, economic and even social environment are not conceived of as material for the enterprise of change. They are givens. The attempt to change the given order of things is seen as futile, a waste of time. Change itself comes to be viewed negatively. Changes are disrup-tions and so are negative in form; and changes are so often negative in content, too. A flood, a diagnosis of cancer, an economic depres-sion all reinforce the concept that the environment is beyond con-trol and that the best that can be hoped for is no change at all.

Talk aimed at changing things, then, is often unintelligible. Things are not ours to change. But often it is more than unintelligi-ble: it can be debilitating. For people who must bear the unbeara-ble, the thought that their situation is not their doing nor is it subject to their correction is somehow liberating and strengthening. It is easier to face fate than our own failures. In her moving book *Return to Laughter*[2], Elenore Smith Bowen speaks of the capacity to keep going she found in the African bush tribe she had gone to study and had come to admire.

> In an environment in which tragedy is genuine and frequent, laughter is essential to sanity. . . . These people were not individ-ually callous; they were weather-beaten by their constant expo-sure to disease and famine. . . . The chief's daughter would reject the cripple. . . . The cripple looked into the mirror of scorn held up for him by the chief's daughter and saw himself through her eyes. (His) song cursed the witches who had made him so and mocked himself for exposing himself to mockery. Then with his own eyes he looked at himself and found something better than her picture and worse than his hopes. 'Thus it is,' his song ended, 'and what can one do?' These people had developed none of the sciences or arts of civilization. They had not learned to change that which is, to wish for a better life so greatly that they would stake the familiar good that might be lost with the familiar evil. They were not, as we are, greedy for the future. We concern ourselves with the reality of what is, because we wish to direct change wisely, hoping thus to preserve the good on which we are agreed while yet attaining what we believe should be. They did not seek to learn thus purposely. If they knew a grim reality, it was because their fate rubbed it into their very souls.

Let me summarize what has been said about change in the small

church world so far: the goal of small church behavior is maintenance not transformation, preservation not change. The small
church world is essentially fixed and unchangeable. When change
does occur it is often disruptive and harmful and so gives a negative
feeling to the very concept of change. And if things are difficult, to
add to the burden of endurance the burden of responsibility for
change is often crushing not liberating.

With these attitudes and perceptions, change, progress, improvement seem to be virtually impossible in the small church. (As one
small church pastor, fresh out of seminary, put it, "Get me out of
here. I didn't become a pastor to be a chaplain to the status quo.")
Is the small church static to the point of being stagnant? Must it be
so? Is leadership nothing but hand-holding because the world is un-
movable?

How is change understood in the small church? First of all,
change is understood in terms of a state or condition not a set of
activities or programs. Suppose a large church pastor were asked to
document a claim that his or her parish had improved in the area
of mission. Increases in mission giving or a litany of new mission
programs would be presented. No one would argue or fail to be
impressed. To the same question a small church person might respond,

> Well, I don't know. We just seem to be more mission-minded
> lately. I think it goes back to the time the Native American girl
> our ladies group had supported for years worshipped with us
> on her way to college. The sincerity in her voice as she said
> 'Thanks' just made us all feel so good. Ever since it just seemed
> that mission was not something outside of us that we should be
> doing, but a real part of us.

Secondly, in the small church the world is not seen as either
static or in flux. Rather it is seen as moving in a sequence of predictable patterns. These patterns can be specified and so may be
seen as "static" to an outside observer, but they feel dynamic from
within. So the ebb and flow of these patterns are seen to be more
permanent than individual life and living them out constitutes our
individual journey. This may seem an abstract formulation but it is
incarnated in very real ways in small church life. This came home
to me one day as I tried to solve "the ladies' group problem." When
I first came to the Harbor Church, there was a very active ladies
group called the Sunday School Builders, the SBB for short. The
SSB had 15–20 out at every bi-monthly meeting and were very active in the life of the church. Their average age, though, was well

above 70. As one year turned into another, the Lord started calling our SSB ladies home. After some years they were down to a half dozen, met half as often, and were noticably less active in church life. I started worrying. The SSB had meant so much to the church, we couldn't just let them die. But how to beef them up? Elect a young president? Push for new people to join? Get them to do "exciting" things? After one "turning point" meeting I asked my wife for a report. "Well," she said, "the older ladies just seem to like to talk about old times. And that leaves the younger ones not knowing what to do." Finally I asked the most straightforward SSBer how things were going with the group. Her answer floored me.

> Well, I don't know why the younger women are coming. It is not meant for them. When I first came to the Island, the older ladies had their group, the EMRO Society, you know. They are all gone now. We younger ladies started the SSB to help build up the Sunday School for the kids. We were the young mothers of the church, now we're grandmothers! But we've had a good time for 45 years. Soon we'll all be gone. Why don't the younger ladies start their own group?

Change was seen as the birth, life and death of the group. The idea of changing the nature of the group to live forever was unnatural and unsatisfying to her.

This leads us to the third aspect of change in the small church world. Change here is understood as growth, development, the fulfilling of potential, the working out of all the bugs. Small church people do not live for change. But small church people do change as they live. "What's New" can honestly be answered most of the time by "Not Much." Nevertheless, small church people go through transitions and transformations over time. In general, they are not greedy for these changes, though. They aren't overly interested in the latest "pop" book nor do they tend to chase all over after the most vibrant sharing group. Rather they see spiritual growth as unfolding naturally. It seems to be tied to the very sequence of life. "When I was a child, I thought as a child" writes the Apostle Paul. "But when I became a man, I put away childish things." We may illustrate some possible touchstones of this sequence: dependency (0–20 yrs), energy (20–40), maturity (40–60), generativity (60 +). One is not likely to jump the steps as one might skip a grade. Nor can one accelerate the process any more than, by thinking, one could add a cubit to one's height. One could jump off the track (e.g., through alcoholism or choosing a life of crime) or one could suspend progress by making immature decisions or living an unvirtuous life. We can make decisions which frustrate our growth. But we don't grow by chasing after it. It is after all God's free and gracious gift. A virtuous life (honesty, hard work, Christian faithfulness, dependability, constancy, compassion, charity) are both evidences of one's being on track and of openness to life's next step. Change is understood as development, growth, maturation. And development is understood as an unfolding of the patterns of life. Both a folk society and a "rational mentality" utilize the concept of journey to describe changes and progress. However the folk mentality understands this as movement along a predefined path. The rational mentality, however, sees this movement as a journey into the unknown.

In the folk mentality, the attaining of goals is not a rational, volitional, existential exercise. The patterned changes are well within the very essence of life and are occasioned by being open to life. Yet, we do make decisions. No understanding of life without decision points can be considered complete. How does the folk mentality deal with this contradiction? It does so, I believe, by stylizing, ritualizing, and institutionalizing the existential decision. The decision for spiritual birth has its own methodology (e.g., sinners' bench and altar calls), language (e.g., born again), music (e.g., "Just As I Am"), and rituals (e.g., immersion). It is almost as if all existential decisions have been collapsed into this one so that we can go about the business of life without further disruption. Compare this resolution to the well-educated, rational, sophisticated, guilt-ridden suburbanite who knows him or herself in the quest for existential authenticity. For this one to decide is to live. To change is to be. Ministry approaches that are effective will vary widely between these two "mentalities."

The Concept of "Fit" in Small Church Ministry

Is it impossible, then, in such a world to do anything new, to make any change for the better, to do something other than what our forefathers did? The answer lies between a definite "Yes!" and a debilitating "No." I believe that a wise small church leader (maybe some pastors, too) can nurture into being behaviors that constitute further movement toward faithfulness. But those actions are not idiosyncratic and arbitrary. No matter how appropriate a ministry seems to the pastor, no matter how "called" one feels to accomplish a particular service, no matter how necessary such a ministry may be to the community, unless it "fits" with the parish, it will amount to nothing over time. Each summer I watched hundreds of thousands of tourists disembark from the ferry boats and flood our little island. What a ministry awaits us here, I thought. Our church, so centrally located in the harbor area, could become a bearer of God's light to countless people. Truly God was bringing our mission field to us. In order to minister, I devised a coffee house program and a summer concert series. I recruited some helpers (usually some lonely Christian college kids), decorated the place, lined up the musicians (fed, housed and transported them, also), passed out publicity, and generally made it work. And it worked for a while, but as soon as I stopped putting inordinate amounts of my own personal energy into it, these programs came grinding to a halt. I was discouraged. Why had so few of my parishioners caught the vision? Had they no concept of mission, of faithfulness, of outreach? Were they such poor Christians as that? While I pondered the failure of these programs, very quietly, some other ministries came into being. Out of a lay led Bible Study came the idea of holding a monthly luncheon for our elder neighbors. Eight years later this "Second Wind" luncheon is still going strong. It has no budget, no church appointed leader, no official staff, no rules for who should attend. Somehow every month food and people appear and it happens. Or, similarly, at one of our Men's Prayer Breakfast meetings, one of the men expressed his concern for certain impoverished neighbors. They needed just a little more to get by with the inflated prices of island commodities. Touched, we each reached into our pockets and he collected $41. Since that day, by word of mouth, church offerings, benefit concerts, anonymous donations, tens of thousands of dollars have been raised and distributed. There is effort expended but no administrator. There is sacrifice but, oh, so much greater blessing. Or again, Project Harvest Share was born when a lay person realized that his excess tomatoes and zucchinis could fill the stomachs of his shut-in neighbors. Now from late summer through fall, vegetables and canned goods appear at church on Sunday and are quietly distributed around to the needy on Monday. Ministry and service? Absolutely! The ones I envisioned, planned, and promoted? Absolutely not. They were the ones that grew out of the congregation's own concerns. They were the ones that "fit."

The small church congregation is concerned. It does want to do mission. It does believe in outreach. But it has a particular way of understanding and acting in this area. It is not motivated by the extent of human need. It is motivated by the proximity of human need. It doesn't know how to give to a faceless person somewhere else, worthy as he may be. But it will bend over backwards to help its "own." It feels uncomfortable in adopting new behaviors. New ministries are like a foreign language, not only different but threatening and debilitating. Yet doing what it already knows how to do for those whom it can get to is as natural as apple pie. Neighborhood surveys, census data, and other objective indices of ministry potential are irrelevant to the small church. But it would be erroneous to conclude that the small church doesn't care about outreach. Their caring is not motivated or revealed in the way it is in a bureaucratic approach, yet it is truly there. The wise leader who would enhance the doing of mission has but to assist his/her small church in putting its feelings into action. So that deed may fit compassion. For example, consider the response in our parish when a valued member of our congregation has become like an irresponsible child in his aging. It hurts us to see him thus and it hurts us more to know the anguish and effort his wife is undergoing to continue to care for him. Many parishioners asked me what could be done. I did not know. Calls offering help were politely rejected. No one knew what to do. Finally, a parishioner made a list of people who would visit for the afternoon or take the husband for a ride, freeing the wife to rest, go shopping, or just be by herself. Everyone was willing to sign up and with such enthusiasm as to make a blessing out of assigning afternoons. The wife appreciated this structure and for weeks now it has gone on, ministry and appreciation, service and blessing. It fit. It released the concern we all felt into a viable way of acting. After all, visiting and driving are what we'd do anyhow. Now we do it for love. All that was needed was a form to give our caring actuality. So if you, small church leader, would like to enhance the caring behavior of your church, do not look for mission programs or data or facts or figures. Look until you find the concern that is already in your people's hearts. And then find a familiar, comfortable way to release it, embodying it in service. Make the service fit the concern.

Conclusion

In this chapter I have attempted to paint a picture of what the world looks like to people in the small church. In doing so I have made the assumption that they exhibit a "folk mentality" and that their social dynamics are like the "folk society" as described by Robert Redfield. Much of my description is hypothetical, inferential and anecdotal. Nevertheless, I feel that it is substantially accurate. There is probably no small church or small church person who sees the world exactly as I have described. Conversely, many large congregations and large church folk may look at the world with some of these elements. Yet I believe I have specified a number of parameters of "folk mentality" which differ markedly from our dominant cultural mentality and so can be used as an "ideal type" for better understanding what makes an actual small church tick.

The parameters of this mentality include the following: Life experience is understood as a totality. The social world, the flow and rhythms of time, the aspects of one's behavior all cohere in an integrated pattern. This pattern provides a solution to the recurrent issues of life, gives one a sense of all being right in the world, and motivates individuals to maintain it. Behavior is motivated more from habit than intention, and changes, though difficult to achieve, can be very long lived. Reflection is not an ordinary behavior. If an explanation is obtainable, it is usually in the form of myth, the story of a particular individual's deeds in the past. Problems are solved but more on the basis of intuition than analysis. Solutions tend to look like the past, be recognized by an inner light going on, and fit the social experience of the people involved. The world is above all a peopled world. All reality is perceived in personal and relational ways. Time is understood as events; it is cyclical and yet is aimed toward the past. Space is not quantitative but is valued for social function and as a point of connection with those who have occupied it. Behavior is aimed at maintaining one's social world and the environment is seen as essentially fixed.

If these characteristics are substantially accurate, as I obviously believe they are, the conclusions for leadership seem bleak indeed. That is if leadership is seen as greater than management. I am using "management" to mean exercising routine decisions which are already within the thought and behavioral patterns of the social entity. Leadership means rather to introduce a movement in the patterns of the group in the direction of greater "match" between its environment and its integrity. Thus leadership involves change. The decision to plant corn due to depletion of prey for a nomadic, hunting tribe is "leadership." How can one lead in a social entity that is structured to resist change? How can one lead in such an entity when the tools of leadership derived from socialization and education are designed for organizations which view change positively? What are some leadership tools and approaches which are appropriate to the small church world? In the next section we will address ourselves to these questions.

CHAPTER IV

The Feel of Leadership: Understandings and Attitudes for Effective Leadership in the Small Church

> Do not be conformed to this world but be transformed by the renewal of your mind, that you may prove what is the will of God, what is good and acceptable and perfect. (Romans 12:2)

One of the hardest transitions for ambitious and well-trained people who would be *small church* leaders is the mental one. It is hard to view the small church world as legitimate, as having a different integrity, a validity of its own, once one has been "conformed" to rational, future oriented, programmatic and quantitative thinking. But all who would understand and lead effectively in folk societies must be "transformed." Anthropologist Elman R. Service describes this transition in his field study:

> "That's-the-way-we-do." Hearing this again was too much. I rose painfully from the squat that I assumed in imitation of my Havasupai friend when he was giving me instruction. I stomped around on my prickling legs and said in near exasperation, "But why?"
>
> Paya looked up at me, silent, and I saw that I was discourteous to the old man by towering over him. I squatted and waited. Everything always took so long! He watched my face as though to be sure of my full attention. I looked into his eyes—watching, waiting.
>
> The silence lingered, except for the sound of the falls and rapids as Havasu Creek rushed through its red-walled gorge toward the Grand Canyon. As usual, we had walked along the stream to be alone for our daily interview, away from his family and neighbors.
>
> Finally, never blinking, his seamed face calm, Paya repeated, "That's-the-way-we-do." He spoke even more slowly than usual. His normal English was halting, with dreamy spaces often conveying as much significance as his words. This illiterate old man

prized exactly expressed thought, and he did not care how long it took to achieve it: the attitude of a respected wise-man. But this phrase, spoken so softly, held me in the same way that his unwavering gaze had stilled my movements.

My introduction to Havasupai culture was also an introduction to the mind of this man, and at first I was never sure which was which. Later I realized that his careful intensity of manner stemmed from concern that I, a messenger to the outside, should understand the ways of the Havasupai—not just his own. "The way *we* do."

I discovered still later that he was trying to teach me a simple idea of great significance, which I have tried to teach others for the past twenty-five years.

In our sessions he would describe in annoying detail how to do a curing ceremony, or plant corn, recite an origin myth, or calculate kinship. I dutifully took down the information, but impatiently. This was my first fieldwork; I wanted some short cuts, generalizations; above all, I wanted to know the reasons *why* the Indians acted in their peculiar ways. Paya answered: "That's-the-way. . . ." Then he would go back to the description as if I had misunderstood the whole thing.

I was looking for a key to Havasupai culture, afraid of not finding it, and right there I impatiently overlooked the truth: *There is no key to understanding another culture except on its own terms.*[1]

The small church, too, must be understood on its own terms, not on our society's or our denomination's or the business world's. It is precisely this transition that is a prerequisite for effective small church leadership. In this section I will attempt to paint in broad strokes some of the insights and understandings (eventually leading to certain kinds of action—as we will see in the next section) which are necessary to a valid ministry in the small church world.

1. Uphill or Downhill?

A new small church pastor should not expect to make significant change immediately and easily nor by virtue of simply being "the pastor." Most of us have been raised to think that we can make a difference. We are educated to think in terms of possibilities. We live in a society which is experiencing rapid flux. Change is rapid, pervasive and accelerating. One isn't "with it" unless one is either creating change or managing it.

The college I went to boasted that it pumped out one thousand leaders every year. Now leaders are those who make a difference, who affect their environment in some significant way. Leaders change things. So I sallied forth not only ready to change the world but thinking that the world was ready to be changed. I was soon to be enlightened on both points! The first few years in my parish I was able to add a number of complementary programs and restore some previous activities. Yes, I was able to change some things, but I was not able to make some fundamental changes in our congregation's priorities and ways of doing things. Sometimes it seemed that the only change I had effected was an increase in the congregation's ability to resist change! How much anguish I could have been spared had I expected resistance instead of readiness.

The small church world does not change easily. Nurturing progress in a small church is a difficult job. It takes time. It takes love. It takes blood, sweat and tears. If you aspire to move a small church congregation be prepared to perspire.

I have a one sentence goal for both my parish's mission commitment and my pastoral ministry efforts. It is: to participate with God in the transformation of human life from its present state toward the individual, corporate and institutional fullness of our divine destiny. "Individual, corporate and institutional" remind me to keep broad and balanced in my concern for faithfulness and rightousness. "To participate with God" keeps me humble! It reminds me that only as God is at work will true progress be made. I can be a channel but not a source of eternity becoming real here and now.

And "the transformation of human life" keeps me on track. The goal of ministry is not production. It is not running programs, raising funds, building buildings. The goal of our ministry is the transformation of human beings (including myself!) Production can be defined and monitored. Transformation can only be glimpsed and nurtured. Production can be scheduled. Transformation is born in eternity and enters our experience in ways we can't predict or control. Production can be accomplished quickly. Transformation takes a long time.

The desire to accomplish a lot quickly results in no lasting effect. There is a pond near our house which our family uses for boating and bathing. When boating I repeatedly push against the waters of the pond with the oars. This, I have noticed, has very little effect on the pond—a few short-lived ripples, not even a hole where the oar once was. Of course, this pushing moves *the boat* (while keeping it *above* the water). But the pond remains unchanged.

We also bathe in the pond. We splash in, swim out over our

heads, feel its buoyancy, warmth and refreshment. From this position we have made some changes in the pond, cleared away some
weeds, raked the rocks away from a ten-foot beach, made it more
inviting. But it took a while and we had to get our feet wet to do it.
It is the same in the small church. One can pastor energetically,
rapidly, from above, make a few waves which have no lasting effect
except to move oneself along. Or one can lead from within, by loving, by giving oneself to the "pond."

I know a pastor who moved his congregation out of the back
pews and down to the front of the sanctuary where he preached
from a small lectern. He accomplished this move in one week. One
week, really? I asked him. Yep. One week. "'Course it took me
twelve years to build up the trust and the sense of mutuality to allow it to happen!"

God doesn't seem to be in a hurry. If after 2000 years God is
still working on transforming humankind, what do we really think
we can accomplish in one week, one month, one year? Maybe we
should think more in terms of generations.

The small church is an inertial organization, not an intentional
one. It goes merrily along in the direction in which it is heading,
not necessarily in the direction we think it ought to be going. This
built-in inertia makes it difficult to change directions. But it is also
the reason why it has survived for so long against difficult odds. It
does not live on the level of rationality and decision making. It lives
on the level of habit and the heart.

Effective leadership in the small church can be very difficult,
takes time, and can best be accomplished from within. The wise
small church leader realizes that to be effective he or she must be
in it for the long haul. And the small church leader realizes, too,
that change in the small church, difficult in all events, is possible
only from within.

2. In or Out?

The wise small church leader must be able to live in and enjoy the
small church world but must not be trapped in it. He or she must
be part of the people in order to have his or her leadership accepted and appropriate, but not so much a part of the small church
world as to offer no impetus to greater faithfulness.

The Doctor of Ministry program in which I was enrolled required me to define a "ministry issue." After writing up the nature
of this problem, its history, causes, etc., I was to share it with a
committee from the congregation. We weren't five minutes into this

session when I noticed Barbara was frowning. Barbara was chairing the Deacons that year. She had been a Trustee for over a decade. She organized almost every social function at the church. What Barbara didn't know about the church wasn't worth knowing. So when Barbara frowned, I frowned. Then her frown deepened. The more she read, the more she frowned. She looked discouraged and then visibly upset. I started to worry. Had I been way off base in my assessment of the needs in the church? Had I been too heavy handed in my description of the problem? "Barbara, what's the matter? Am I wrong in the way I have sized things up?" she paused and sighed. "No. No, it's all true. I just hate to see it in black and white."

For Barbara our church is like family. We have problems, certainly. And we are aware of them. We know them in our heart and in our gut. We live with them. We change what we can. But we don't think of them in a detached, clinical, objective way, as if we could divorce the problem from ourselves. We have met the problem, and it is us, to paraphrase Pogo. And we certainly don't tell the neighbors about it. That would be going too far.

In writing up our church's problems for the seminary, I had gone over the line. In expressing objectively what we all knew subjectively, I had placed myself outside of the identity of the group. I had put myself over against them. This was not a welcome activity. It threatened the group, and Barbara was sensitive and honest enough to express it. My movement from pastor, inside the small church, to critic, outside the group, exposed their vulnerability. It laid bare their frailties and foibles, and, had I persisted, it would have led to "irrational" behavior on their part to defend themselves from me. "I was afraid because I was naked; so I hid." (Genesis 3:10).

This response of threat and defensiveness sometimes occurs when no criticism is communicated or even intended. It occurs when changes ("improvements"), such as new mission programs, are suggested by one not central to the group. The response is not to weigh objectively the proposal—need, resources, and calling—to see if we ought to proceed. Rather the response is "What's the matter—we're not good enough for you as we are?" Or "Take us as you find us." Or "Pay your dues before you nominate yourself president." Or maybe there is no verbal response (or possibly even a mild positive one), but in a thousand and one ways the new program is resisted and/or sabotaged. So that who we are is indicated in its failing! "We told you it wouldn't work." Or, "We tried that once before." "See, we were right all along." It is seldom productive to threaten the identity of the group.

And yet a faithful small church leader must not equate the Kingdom of God with the present state of his congregation. He or she cannot live completely within the little world of the small church and be true to one's calling as pastor. The small church leader must be able to "step out" once in a while, to look Biblically and objectively at his or her tribe, to set one's sights on God's intentions for the congregation. But then the effective small church leader needs to step back inside the small church world. Certain prophets of Israel were able to weigh the tribes on the scale of eternity. They found Israel wanting. They stepped out but they didn't step back in. They became literally a voice crying in the wilderness. Their pleas are as appropriate today as they were originally, possibly because they had so little success in getting anybody to see things their way.

The faithful small church leader must not self-righteously march into the role of external critic—little true ministry occurs from that position—nor slip into the small church world so totally as to lose sight of eternity. The faithful small church leader must live with a tension most of his or her people will not have to live with. The faithful small church leader must live inside *and* outside of the small church world. He or she must live with one foot in each world.

3. Backward or Forward?

One of the small prop planes that flies to Block Island is a six seater with the two middle seats facing backward. This creates a cozy foursome for conversation during the 15-minute flight from the mainland. Nevertheless, I avoid these rear facing seats if at all possible. Why? Because I find it disorienting and uncomfortable to not be facing where I am going. I don't like to be looking at where I've been. I want to be keyed in on where I'm heading. I like to have my sights set on my goals. The Forward Look. This is what progress and leadership are all about.

However, there are two problems with the Forward Look for small church leaders. One is that it is not how life is actually lived. And two is that small church people find it an uncomfortable way to live life. For some reason best known only to the Divinity, God has created time (as opposed to space) to be unidirectional. We can know the happenings of the past, but we cannot know with certainty the future. We do move forward in time but we don't really know where we are going. We can plan, prepare, predict, pro-act, but we can never know where we will be until we've gotten there. Intentionality, goal setting, strategizing are means of making desirable potential outcomes more probable. But we only *know* where we have been. We can only be certain of the past. The Backward Look is the only perspective that sees reality. The Forward Look is an "illusion" based on intention. It may create a reality, but it is not a reality. We can only move forward in time on the basis of the past, on the basis of history and experience.

Not only is the Backward Look reality, but small church people are comfortable with this reality. The past is their home. Tradition is their method of operating. "The way we have done things before" is the way we want to do them. Small church people know these ways, feel comfortable with these ways, see these as "the right" ways, and know themselves as the enactors of these ways.

In the abstract of Redfield's "Folk Society" he describes the content of the article:

> Such a society is small, isolated, nonliterate, and homogeneous, with a strong sense of group solidarity. The ways of living are conventionalized into that coherent system which we call "a culture." Behavior is traditional, spontaneous, uncritical, and personal, there is no legislation or habit of experiment and reflection for intellectual ends. Kinship, its relationships and institutions, are the type categories of experience and the familial group is the unit of action. The sacred prevails over the secular; the economy is one of status rather than of the market. These and related characterizations may be restated in terms of "folk mentality."[2]

So the Folk society is seen in a small grouping of people who know each other well. They have a past which includes each other. Their history is a shared history. Therefore one aspect of their past is its personal nature. The past that is functional in the folk society is limited because the pure folk society is non-literate and has little contact with other peoples. So the past is what is remembered in the minds and the oral traditions of its members. Furthermore, the past becomes present reality in the "culture" of the folk people.

> The ways in which the members of the society meet the recurrent problems of life are conventionalized ways; they are the results of long intercommunication within the group in the face of these problems and these conventionalized ways have become interrelated within one another so that they constitute a coherent and self-consistent system. Such a system is what we mean in saying that the folk society is characterized by "a culture." A culture is an organization or integration of conventional understandings. It is, as well, the acts and the objects, in so far as they represent the type characteristic of that society, which express

and maintain these understandings. In the folk society this integrated whole, this system, provides for all the recurrent needs of the individual from birth to death and of the society through the seasons and the years.[3]

The way in which things are done in a folk society is another way in which the past is determinative of the present.

What is done in the ideal folk society is done not because somebody or some people decided, at once, that it should be done, but because it seems "necessarily" to flow from the very nature of things. There is, moreover, no disposition to reflect upon traditional acts and consider them objectively and critically. In short, behavior in the folk society is traditional, spontaneous, and uncritical.[4]

Further, the way in which the past has determined the present goes a long way toward shaping the future. "The interrelations and high degree of consistency among the elements of custom which are presented to the individual declare to him the importance of making his endeavors in the direction indicated by tradition."[5]

In addition, the ways of the past are not only comfortable, but they came to be endowed with a moral rectitude above and beyond their functionality.

The ways of life are folkways; furthermore, the folkways tend to be also mores—ways of doing or thinking to which attach notions of moral worth. The value of every traditional act or object or institution is, thus, something which the members of the society are not disposed to call into question; and should the value be called into question the doing so is resented. This characteristic of the folk society may be briefly referred to by saying that it is a sacred society. In the folk society one may not, without calling into effect negative social sanctions, challenge as valueless what has come to be traditional in that society.[6]

We have in Redfield's description a society which operates in a very short time frame (unto the third and fourth generations), whose past is preserved by means of oral traditions, habituated behavior and conventionalized thought patterns brought into the present in such a way as to almost make a unity of the two, and whose future looks very much like a mirror image of its past-present. In such a society the past becomes the present and predicts the future by means of some combination of folk traditions and oral history, myth-sharing, story telling, habitual behavior and conventionalized world view. It is particularly important for us to note the degree to which moral rightness and sacredness inhere in the past-made-present. What this means is that the past, our traditions, are not only the way we are today, but are also the way we must be. Excepting an utterly debilitating crisis situation, it appears as though change and renewal are hardly possible in such a society.

What can we conclude about renewal and the past in this kind of society? We may conclude, first of all, that change is very difficult to achieve in such a social entity. It will be resisted as not only alien but also as immoral, as indeed, from an internal perspective, it is. But to the degree that renewal, adaptation and change are possible, they cannot be conceived as occurring through a rational attempt to apprehend the future. Rather, they must come as aspects of the past. It must sound like what we believed all along and it must look like who we have been all along.

However comfortable and appropriate the Backward Look may be for small church people, it is not an adequate perspective for leadership. Only in the case of a social grouping perfectly adapted to a static environment would looking backward only be an adequate leadership style. I doubt that such a case has ever existed and it certainly does not exist for today's small church leader. Effective leadership in the small church today must be able to look forward. Such leaders must be able to perceive social and demographic trends. Such leaders must register changes within the congregation itself. Such leaders must be alert to new needs and hurts in their communities. Such leaders must hear anew the voice of Christ calling in the "least of these my brethren."

But such a leader must not expect to persuade anybody in their small church to respond on the basis of such a Forward Look. Rather one can expect the Forward Look to be disorienting and debilitating. To the degree that it is registered, it feels like a lament, not a call. "Things aren't the way they used to be (in the good old days)." "I hardly know anybody here any more." (A comment overheard after the pastor welcomed six new people into membership in a small church!)

The Forward Look is the function of leadership, not of the whole body of the small church. Having looked forward, the effective small church leader's job has just begun. He or she must now step back into the world of history and heritage, memory and tradition. He or she must scan the past for values and behaviors which are appropriate for the future. These he must cultivate and nurture. Thus will she lead forward by utilizing the Backward Look of the congregation.

This is a significantly different enterprise than planning in a rational organization. It embodies different values. It utilizes different strategies. The effective small church leader must be willing to live with a sprained neck, but he must not think he can lead by looking forward only.

4. Reflexive or Reflective?

The effective small church leader needs to disabuse himself or herself of two notions of leadership. The first is that a small church pastor sits atop the congregation the way a general sits atop his troops. The small church is not a pyramid of power with the pastor at the apex. "Orders" barked by small church pastors are much more likely to be disobeyed or ignored than obeyed. "Lording it over" Christ's followers is not a faithful leadership posture.

Neither is the opposite assumption, that is, that the body of believers of themselves will respond adequately to ensure their internal health and external mission, without leadership activity. The small church as we have argued is an "inertial" organization. It will keep on going in a pre-set direction virtually in isolation from the movement of the environment. Over time these two movements result in a mis-match between the church and its field unless adjustments are accomplished.

Furthermore, in a folk society it is much easier to forget behavior than it is to learn new ones. Therefore the repertoire of behaviors available to a small church decreases over time unless new behaviors are introduced. This was driven home to me regarding hymn singing in my parish. The church had a hymnal which was unfamiliar to me at the time I became the pastor. When I selected a hymn, known to me but new to the congregation, the complaints after the service were much louder than the singing of the hymn. Precious little effort was made to acquaint me with "our favorites," nor did I attempt to compile such a list on my own. Instead, I shied away from picking hymns unknown to myself lest they were also unknown to the congregation—this lead to the worst of both worlds: negative reaction from the parish and the absence of the joy and comfort which would ordinarily be engendered by familiar lyrics and tunes. Consequently, we were singing from a very narrow band of hymns—a great loss for all of us. Eventually, realizing this dynamic, I moved to overcome it. But that is the point. The natural dynamics of an inertial organization lead to diminution. Leadership activity is necessary to keep open to God's riches.

How are we to understand the nature of this activity and its dynamics? Consider a simple model drawn from biology.

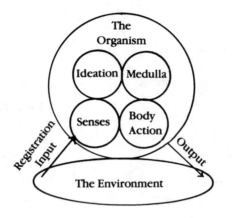

The environment is the world beyond the small church per se. Frequently this is, effectively, the community or neighborhood, the denomination, and particular sets of relationships that have developed over time. Inputs (changes, resources, etc.) are registered by the small church. The locus of this registration I am depicting as the sensory function of the small church. The brain is the locus of ideational response, typically, rational, logical, future-oriented, programmatic. The medulla may for our purposes be considered the locus of "instinct." It is the place where spontaneous, uncritical, unreflective impetus for action originates. The body is the arms, hands, legs, lips, ears, etc., that actually minister to the world. This is the agency of output into the environment, the "doers of the word."

The two disfunctional leadership postures may be diagrammed as:

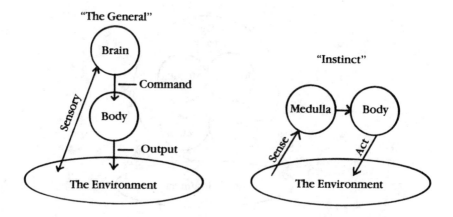

What I presume to be a model for a healthy large church is:

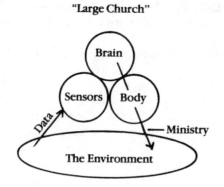

What I would propose for the small church looks like this:

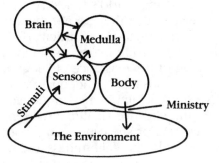

(Note: These models are meant to be evocative of differing leadership approaches. They are not meant to be pushed regarding detail.)

The small church is a primarily reflexive, not a reflective organization. It senses needs in the environment and responds in ways that have proved effective and meaningful in the past. In the vast majority of cases this is very helpful and efficient. It does a lot of good quickly and comfortably because both giver and receiver have come to expect that type of help. In our parish, for example, it is not uncommon for me to go to the hospital on the mainland to visit a sick parishioner or islander and find the wall of their hospital room literally covered with get well cards. "It is so, so encouraging," they say with tears in their eyes, "to know so many people are thinking of me and praying for me. It does my heart good." Our card mailing is a reflexive ministry—we don't invent it each time, it is just part of who we are and how we express our love. And we have many more: after-funeral luncheons, Christmas caroling, shut-in visitations, seniors' luncheons, etc. Christ's love is made real in every one of these ways.

But not all ministry is as it has been since our forefathers slept. Someone has speculated that more change has occurred in the twentieth century than in all the previous centuries combined. The situation is a-changing. New needs and ministry opportunities are arising. The faithful small church will be called to minister to a

changing community. But how can it do something that is not reflexive?

The effective small church leader knows that he is working with
a reflexive organization. And she also knows she is not dealing with
a primarily reflective one. It is not that small church people do not
or cannot think. Some of the world's wisest people are small
church people. Rather it is that they do not think that thinking—
rational, abstracted, impersonal—is a particularly helpful tool for
the solution of life's ongoing life issues. And they may have a
weaker comprehension of the existence of "new" needs (i.e., those
for which reflexive solutions are not adequate), or they may be
fearful—an intuitive sense of impotency in the face of "new" problems. Here is where the effective small church leader can function
for greater faithfulness. He or she can dream about new behaviors
that will result in greater health, faithfulness and ministry in the
congregation. But—and this is most important—if those dreams are
to become reality and live over time as a ministry of the congregation, they must become *reflexes*. The small church is not interested
in reinventing its ministries at each annual business meeting. It understands faithfulness not as "being intentional" (in its current fad-
dish and obnoxious sense), but as being constant. So new and
appropriate ministry programs need to become part of our identity,
part of who we are.

This function of leadership—the creation of new responses, behaviors, reflexes—is a sometime, indirect, and hidden activity. It is
sometime, not regular. It is like salt, delicious as a seasoning,
ghastly as a main course! It should be engaged in as needed—to
respond to a new situation, correct an oversight or weakness, etc.
But to think that the small church can be rationally redesigned periodically is to misunderstand completely its nature. Second, it is indirect in that, for maximum effectiveness over time, it must become
a reflex, not simply an activity. This requires a shift in focus from
the product (ministry) to the producer (ministers). Pushing to
achieve an outcome is a one-time enterprise. Building a new reflex
within the life of the people is a slower, less straightforward, but
more satisfying activity. It can sometimes be accomplished by "clon-
ing"—eliciting a behavior which is very similar to an existing behavior—or "kaleidoscoping"—rearranging a set of familiar behaviors into a new ministry pattern. And third, it is a hidden activity. It
cannot be done with trumpets and fireworks. The quieter, simpler,
and more behind the scenes its development, the more likely is its
success. And the more limited the role of the initiator, the more
likely is its long-term viability. The leader who senses a need, creates a solution, and implements the ministry on his own is more

likely to be burned out than beneficial. The response to a need that is widely felt and broadly enacted out of generalized concern is well on its way to being a reflex.

Programs can be credited to creators, reflexes must be everyone's child. I learned this the hard way. I once proposed a Sunday School addition on the south wall of our Fellowship Hall. It was soundly and noisily rejected at our annual meeting. I got more "guff" for that proposal than for any ten of my other best "worst ideas." "Tony's addition" became a byword of ridiculousness. Time went by. Finally, the proposal was forgotten. But the issue remained—where to put our growing Sunday School? The Trustees considered various options. The addition was put on the list. Less feasible alternatives withered. The addition remained. Finally, it was deemed the best. It was duly explained by the Trustees and approved overwhelmingly at our annual meeting four years after it was derisively rejected. In those four years it had been forgotten that I proposed it. It had been forgotten how unfeasible it once seemed. It had gone from a foolish, impossible idea to an idea, to a good idea, to the best idea. No one remembers that it was my idea. And that's fine—since the Sunday School got the space they needed. In fact, someone brought up how 25 years ago a trustee subcommittee came up with the idea!

5. Spear Waving or Sticking to the Subject?

In *Return to Laughter,* anthropologist Elenore Smith Bowen recounts her experiences among the tribesmen of the bush in Africa. Her description of how conflict is resolved and how decisions are made is fascinating and insightful.

> There was a long wait, while more and more elders came. I located Ikpoom. He told me that a woman married into this homestead had died in the night; she had five children; the strangers were her relatives; she would be buried today.... I was prepared for ritual, for funeral orations perhaps, for anything but what actually happened. It was a debate, conducted with all the noise and irreverence of a court case. And I understood not one word of it. First the strangers orated. Kako and his elders objected to everything they said. The strangers spoke even more hotly. En masse, they advanced to the center of the yard. The notables...marched grimly out into the yard. Old men stuck out their chins pugnaciously; they shouted and waved their barbed spears in menacing gesticulation.... Finally Kako and

some of his elders, either convinced or outshouted, returned to our tree and sat down again. Not Yabo. He, Poorgbilin and a few others were still arguing and brandishing their spears in dangerous persuasion. It looked like the beginning of a fight; I hoped it was merely their style of rhetoric. Kako tried to quiet Yaho, who turned upon him with a snarl. Kako jumped up, backed by his followers. He and Yabo argued bitterly. Meanwhile, the strangers unobtrusively and prudently withdrew to their own tree.[7]

And, on a second occasion:

Yabo and Poorgbilin had the same greatgrandfather. The day's business could not be settled unless all the male descendents of that ancestor were present. They could continue to ostracize Yabo only by slighting their own and pressing business. People here lived so closely together that almost every movement of one irritated another. Yet they were so dependent on each other that continuing a feud or indulging a spite was a luxury taxed with personal disadvantage. Yabo was called to the meeting and came. At first, he was treated to ... cold civility. ...

However, the polite manner is incompatible with their debating technique. One cannot shout and brandish a spear with reserve. Inevitably, as soon as people began to find their interests threatened, they began to stamp and scream. Yabo was out in the middle, yelling with the best of them. It was an angry scene, but a very normal one. Yabo, I felt, was back in.[8]

I have a theological degree from each of two seminaries. For each degree I took work in church administration. In each church administration course the topic of how to handle governing committees or deacon boards was dealt with. Forming agendas, setting priorities, directing discussions, gaining consensus, minimizing diversions, assigning tasks, delegating responsibilities, eliminating tangents were some of the wonderful things I learned how to do. And I found that these things worked reasonably well on a national task force which I chaired. The members of the Task Force met every six months, had little interaction between meetings, weren't exactly sure why we were meeting, didn't know what to expect from our meetings, but were highly task motivated once the meeting was called to order. The Task Force members were, by and large, willing to stick to the subject once it was specified. Of course, it took *three years* to figure out the specification!

The members of my church's governing boards are not confused about why they are meeting. They might not be able to put it into sharp verbal focus, but they know in their hearts. They do not need my administration to stick to the subject. Their life together is the subject. And they stick to it in their own way. But when you live with someone in close proximity week in and week out for decades and with the prospect of decades more, the ways of doing things are different. The task agenda is the lesser agenda. The relationship agenda is the greater concern. Small church people have to live together. They have to live with themselves and with each other. This leads to seemingly contradictory behaviors. In order to live with each other, they have sometimes to go sit under their tree and be quiet, to use Bowen's image. In order to live with themselves, they have to yell and scream, stomp and jump, and wave their spears. But all of this is part of the great dance of living together. It must not be understood as a reaction to content alone.

Spear waving may be "a very angry scene." But it is also "a very normal one." Spear waving has its healthy aspects. It ensures that every position is heard and every ego is accounted for. It clears the air and gives each their say. And it clearly reveals who is invested in the issue, in the church, in the common life. It allows people to move from the emotional agenda to the objective one, from the relational issue to the content one.

The effective small church leader does not fear spear waving. (The two extremes may be cause for concern, though. No spear waving indicates no investment. And excessive spear waving, that which leads to interpersonal violence, need not be tolerated.) Rather, it is seen as a means of allowing people to live together over time. Once spear waving serves its proper cathartic role, leadership can be exerted. Each side can be shown how at least some of their concerns are embodied in the course of action to be taken. Each side can feel that its position was at least heard. Each side may be "spent" enough after the spear waving to heed the leader's temperate approach. It takes leadership abilities beyond agenda-izing. It takes real creativity and sensitivity. It is challenging. But it is fun.

The "Hanging of Nathan Mott" illustrates this dynamic. Nathan Mott was an island sea captain who invested his fortune in a hotel in 1885. Through various bequests that hotel has become our present church building. Some of our members remember Nathan Mott and thought it appropriate that his portrait hang in the church's vestibule. After all, if it were not for Nathan we would not have a church (building). Others wondered for years who that old man hanging in the vestibule was. When the vestibule was repainted Nathan was put away for "safe keeping." After a couple of years his absence was noticed by three of our older ladies. They were seen meeting together to discuss this problem. After a while the Trustee chair was taken to task for displacing this portrait, but he could not see why the picture of Jesus that now hung there was of less importance to the church than Nathan. Finally, after a few more discussions, he agreed to rehang Nathan. He did so, but in a new spot behind the door opening up to the balcony. That would never do for our ladies. It would have to do, according to our Trustee. Level by level the tension mounted, our ladies ever more loudly making their demands, our trustee ever more adamantly denying them. Enter the pastor with a proposal to create a display regarding our whole heritage of faith with the portrait of Nathan one part thereof. Motion approved. Nathan rehung pending the complete display. Now we can sit under our trees until the next time the need to wave our spears arises.

6. Seeing or Believing?

"Seeing is believing," the expression goes. Thomas wouldn't believe that Jesus had been raised from the dead until he saw the imprint of the nails on Jesus' hands and feet. The phrase "I'm from Missouri" conveys much the same idea: I'm not going to believe it until I see it for myself.

But believing leads to seeing just as much as the reverse. Believing in a new reality, envisioning a different future, dreaming of a new tomorrow is often the first step in its realization. Believing is seeing, too.

Most people in the small church though, are from Missouri. With the Apostle John they would say they know that which "we have heard, which we have seen with our eyes, which we have looked upon and touched with our hands" (1 John 1:1). Like Thomas they aren't going to believe anything new until they see it. Things are as they have been. New things are not believed until they have been experienced. Most small church people give credence to their body's eye not their mind's eye. Only a precious few can envision new realities, can hear the Lord calling them forth into a land which they have never seen.

This reality poses a challenge for the small church leader when changes, perceived as more than refinements, are at stake. How can movement be encouraged in this situation?

A revealing incident occurred on our Renovations Committee. I had tried to constitute this committee as broadly and as representatively as possible. Every facet of the life of the church was reflected in this group which was to oversee the remodelling of our fellowship hall, kitchen and Sunday School areas. I figured that whatever we could hammer out would have relatively smooth sailing with the rest of the congregation. But I hadn't figured on how hard it would be to hammer things out in this committee. From the beginning of our discussion on remodelling the kitchen, peculiar behavior occurred. Even though an existing floor plan with two possible remodelings, all drawn to scale, were on blueprints in front of us, people would leave the meeting, walk next door to the kitchen area, and return in a couple of minutes. One by one they went until they had all gone at least once. Then two by two, then groups at a time. The meeting began to resemble musical chairs! Finally, I got up and joined the parade to find that each one was pacing around the kitchen trying to "see" what the proposed changes would really be like! It was obvious that the blueprints did little to help them "see" the new kitchen. Rather they had to go to the spot and "feel" it.

If that got us off to a flying start, the second meeting went downhill from there. Tension filled the air from the opening prayer. Every proposed improvement in the kitchen was objected to, deemed irrelevant, or otherwise resisted. What confounded me was that the one who was objecting the most was the one I figured to benefit the most from the changes. It was the lady who, with great personal effort, organizes the crews to work in the kitchen for our big fund-raising dinners. "I don't see why we need more space. We get along fine as it is." (Workers during big dinners are so tightly packed into our home-sized kitchen that to get another platter of potatoes to serve in the dining hall, a bucket brigade has to be formed, for, literally, not one more person could be squeezed into the kitchen!) "And you can't make that the clean-up area. That's where we serve the cranberry sauce from." The new and efficient cranberry serving spot had gone by unregistered! The problem, the new floor plan and the need for the plan were just plain not seen. Although I desperately wanted her input and blessing of the planned changes, she ceased coming to meetings. "No sense causing a fight." In fact, the whole group shrunk down to an unrepresentative handful who could see where the rub was and could envision ways to change things. Finally the plans were approved and the kitchen renovated. With fear and trepidation I awaited the coming of our first big dinner in the new kitchen. Surprisingly things went without a hitch! The next day the organizer saw me downtown and started flapping her arms in an amazing likeness to a chicken! For the life of me I couldn't figure out what was up. "Didn't the dinner go great?" she asked. "And it was so pleasant having plenty of room to work in." (Thus the arm movements.) Apparently she took my chin dropping to the ground as agreement, and went merrily on her way. She is a wonderful Christian and a very hard worker for Christ's church. She just sees things by experiencing them, not by envisioning them!

I had come into the pastorate believing consensus to be the Christian method of operating. Failing that in important areas, the majority was to rule. How much time I wasted, how much energy I lost, how many feelings I hurt trying to persuade people *before-hand* of a greater good. In fact, it is only by experiencing that a judgment can be made. It is only *after* personal involvement that evaluation can be effected.

Only a very few people in a small church culture can envision the significant new things that God is calling us to—is this what the Apostle Paul means when he says that some have the *gift* of faith? The effective small church leader will not bother with the nearly futile exercise of trying to get all or the majority to agree a priori with a change. Rather he or she will work with the one or two or three who can "see" what is yet to be. When the vision has become tangible enough for the others to "see," it will be incorporated into the body or it will be rejected, just as the human body accepts or rejects an organ. For people who know, not by thinking and projecting, but by experiencing, only at that point can a fair and informed decision be made. The good leader will allow them that input before "calling the question."

In my experience, two further things occur if the change is accepted. One is that a precedent will be found. "Oh, it's nothing new. Not really. Remember when Pastor Time-Out-Of-Mind was here. We did something about the same then. That's when. . .(there follows a story)." The second is that those whose only input was negative become some of the loudest evangelists of the change. The thing they opposed with boundless energy is that of which they are now proud as peacocks! I don't understand this dynamic, but it reminds me of the hockey player who, after giving up the winning goal, praised the scorer. "He has to be a darn good player to get one past me." So it must be a darn good idea to get it past The Preservers of Our Equilibrium!

Summary of Attitudes

Someone once quipped that if you give a person a hammer it is amazing what he will find to pound on. The tools at one's disposal, more than the needs of the situation, determine behavior. The hammer is a great tool, but sometimes a saw or shovel or telescope or word processor is more appropriate to the enterprise. Through our educational activities, our culture, and the potency of the business approach in our society, most of us have been given tools that work in a rationally organized, bureaucratically structured, forward looking organization. To minister effectively in the small church, however, another set of tools is necessary. The attitude and approach of the small church leader is the most basic of his or her leadership tools. To the degree they are in accord with the nature of the small church's social structuring they will be effective. I have described six qualities of the small church and six corresponding attitudes:

1. The small church is a stable, not a dynamic, organization. Its nature is to replicate not rethink its previous patterns of behavior. Therefore the effective small church leader will be aware that change is difficult to achieve and that it will take a long time relative to a rationally structured organization. The effective small church leader will realize that he or she is in it for the long run, will not be discouraged by the pace, but rather will be encouraged by the fact that a new good, once in place, may live "forever."

2. The typical small church is in a "little world to itself." This world is satisfying and meaningful to those within. But it is not self-correcting, nor is it even aware of itself objectively. It is difficult to change from the outside, and it is difficult to determine the path of greater faithfulness to Christ from the inside. Since both of those functions are necessary to effective leadership, such a leader must learn to live with the tension of living both inside and outside the world of the congregation.

3. The typical small church sees the past not the future. It registers what has been, not what can be. However, leadership involves orienting one's people to the future. The effective small church leader must be ready and willing to value the past, not only for its own merit, but also as a tool for the future. Those who are unwilling to look backward in order to move forward had better have a high frustration tolerance.

4. The typical small church functions out of reflex and habit not from goals and strategies, rationally defined. Therefore, ministry in a small church does not so much concern getting the job done as it does building up good habits, ingrained behavioral patterns. The effective small church leader must be comfortable with secondary and indirect activity, transformation not production.

5. The typical small church lives on the level of relationships not tasks. These relationships require work. They must be kept balanced and livable. A lot of energy is expended toward this end. Every serious task proposed by the pastor has not only its own mer-

anced and livable. A lot of energy is expended toward this end. Every serious task proposed by the pastor has not only its own merits but the possibility of upsetting relational balance. Small church people will act in ways which restore homeostasis. The effective small church leader will recognize this for what it is and accept it as a natural and necessary phenomenon. She will act in ways to keep it within bounds and will not lose sight of the task because of it.

6. The typical small church lives on the experiential not the theoretical level. Effective small church leaders will find ways to bring into people's experience the issues before them. They will work with the few who can foresee to bring new things into being. They will be less concerned with the purity of consensus or majority rule than with the practicality of giving their people a taste of what lies before them.

It is obvious in our discussion of attitudes of effective small church leaders that actions are not far away. Let us now turn our attention from the appropriate internal stance of the effective small church leader to behaviors that indicate quality leadership in the small church social situation.

CHAPTER V

Leadership Activities in the Small Church World

"Be doers of the Word, and not hearers only."

(James 1:22)

How can we act, then, as small church lovers and leaders? Here are six action strategies:

1. Horse or Cart?

"Plan the work and work the plan." So the pastor of a medium-sized, suburban church advised me during my seminary field placement. Very wise advice, too. Of course, it is based on the assumption that effort flows from intention. This it did in his parish. Long range planning committees led to new building plans which, in turn, led to new buildings.

But the flow, if there is one, is usually the other way in the small church: behavior leads to its own rationale. Leadership in the small church is not an exercise in rationality but in rationale. Behaviors which are sustained over time in the life of the parish justify themselves by their very presence. Actions are right (for us) if we do them and have done them for time-out-of-mind. A story is told of a small church pastor who desired to introduce a change in the way in which communion was observed. From the Board he requested a six-month trial period for the new ceremony. Feeling, apparently, that this was too brief a period to cause any real harm, the Board approved the request. After the trial period was over, the pastor, very conscientiously, inquired of the Board if they would like to stick with the new ritual. "Huh? What new ceremony? That's the way we've always done it. What else is on your mind, tonight?" Had they really forgotten their old ceremony? Who knows? They were using their memories in service of their identity not the facts. So harmonious was the new ceremony with the life of the parish that it felt as if it had always been with them. "We've always done it that way" is just another way of saying, "It is us." Behavior lead to rationale and acceptance in a way a rational discussion of the two ceremonies never could. Or to put it another way, for small church people theology explains praxis. But the praxis is the important thing. For a change of behavior to be accepted and incorporated in a small church, it must be experienced. It may be rejected after it is experienced, but it will almost certainly be rejected if the only apprehension of it is theoretical.

What does this mean for small church leaders? It means that it is by doing not by discussing that small church people decide about the helpfulness and faithfulness of changes. Two strategies that small church leaders can employ to allow the doing include trial periods and increments. The trial period, as noted above, allows acting without threat. It is like trying on a hat. If it doesn't fit, it is OK to put it back on the shelf. You haven't bought it forever. Increments allow people to get into a new behavior step by step. At a recent workshop I presented these six action strategies. When I finished, one lady let out a sigh. "I'm so concerned about the teenagers in our town," she said. "Many are into drugs in part because they have nothing else to do. But when I proposed to the Trustees to open up the church for a Saturday night dance, I was turned down flat. How can they be so un-Christian?"

It was obvious to me this lady really cared. "Instead of lamenting their faithlessness, let's consider the situation's dynamics from a folk society perspective," I said.

You were asking to introduce a change into the pattern of the church. Change, including discussion thereof, activates fear in the hearts of folk people. Some were probably afraid the building would be misused. Some were afraid of this 'perverse and untoward generation.' Some may have been brought up to view dancing as of the devil. Some may just fear anything different. All these fears, and more, you probably activated by asking for the whole thing at once. My hunch is that few small church people like being pushed into the deep end of the pool. Most stick a toe in, take a step or two in, and then wade in backwards! And who is to say that a dance would have interested the kids you are concerned about? Why not take it a step at a time. Ask for an OK for you and a few kids to use the hall a couple of nights for Monopoly, or whatever, maybe as a part of your youth group program. No Drugs. No Dancing. You'll clean up. No threat. Just a little more of what we're already doing. If it catches on, build it up and invite a trustee each night to help out. If not, you're no worse off than you are with the 'No' you've got now.

I could almost see the light bulb go on in her head!

2. "The Good Old Days"

It seems that for those of us trained in the ways of modernity, the past, tradition, heritage, "the way we've always done it," is an enemy, maybe *the* enemy, or, at best, unnecessary baggage weighing down every forward step. How much more appropriate it would be for us, especially we who name the name of the One who lived two thousand years ago, who look for guidance into a Book started three millenia ago, for us to see the past as an ally, a means of moving into God's future.

The past can provide the effective small church leader grist for moving forward in terms of insight, inspiration, and identity. I would like to tell you about my own journey on this road.

Early in my pastorate I felt myself at a decision point not of my own making. Denomination officials, my parents, even some parishioners were all sending me a message: a good pastor doesn't stay in a small church for long—he pays his dues and then takes a step up the ladder. I felt torn between a conscious desire to succeed and an unconscious desire to stay put and minister, to "progress" not by moving out, but in sticking it out. As this struggle began to increase in intensity, I happened upon *Small Churches Are Beautiful*[1], edited by Jackson Carroll. One of the first essays describes the pastoral situation of colonial New England. I was fascinated and stirred by what I learned. In the past, pastoral status was lodged in one's calling to the ministry not in the quantitative indices of one's parish. The rural, small church pastor and the urban, large church pastor stood on equal ground. In part this was so because pastorates were long—usually a life time! Nearly 80% of colonial pastors served one church all their lives. And the 5% or so who had more than two were considered n'er-do-wells, either troublemakers or bereft of the qualities of perseverance and fortitude. In that moment of "relearning" my past, I gained a tremendous insight into my value framework. I had been basing my self-esteem as a pastor on a 20th century, corporate business model. From the past I was liberated to accept another model, a model based on quality, calling, loyalty, and historical precedent. In that moment I was freed from the debilitation of my internal conflict. I was freed to serve my parish with renewed energy. Over a decade has passed since then and I am still amazed at how far forward I have come because I looked backward. History. Insight. Energy. Ministry.

A number of months ago I was visiting a parish family. In the course of the conversation they casually mentioned a booklet published by our historical society. Which was that? I asked. Hadn't read it? Here, take this extra copy. I did. And my attitude toward my parish and the congregation's attitude toward themselves have never been the same since. Previously I had read some history of the Island, but the origins of the church seemed lost in the mist of time. It had taken the white settlers over a century to get around to founding a church and even then history records mostly construction details. It didn't sound very inspiring. But then I read the booklet *The Real Mystery of BLOCK ISLAND*[2] by Arthur Kinoy, an attorney. Reasoning like a trial lawyer, weaving facts, logic and psychology, Kinoy paints a picture of a struggling band of men of conscience meeting secretly behind closed doors in Boston just after the public lynching of Mary Dyer. These men were bound together by a quest for religious freedom. Against major odds and forsaking their business interests, wealth and social position, they landed on the shores of little Block Island following the siren of liberty. Led by Captain Sands in civic affairs, Simon Ray in spiritual matters, and Trustrum Dodge in the practical aspects of wresting life from an hostile environment, they established not just a viable settlement, but a community of faith based on "soul liberty" and individual conscience. For nearly 100 years, Kinoy relates, Ray and his son Simon, Jr., led home worship, feeding the souls of those daring men, nourishing them in the fight for liberty. By the year Simon Ray Jr., passed on, the forces for national political liberty were on a collison course with England, and the forces were well established, too, which would result in the Bill of Rights. Yes, the settling of Block Island was only a tiny thread, but it was a thread in the Great Tapestry of Freedom. So I, pastor in the succession of men and women who risked all for their conscience and their God. My congregation worships and ministers in the succession of those who forged freedom. To us they have passed the torch. I will hold it high. What an honor and an inspiration it is for us to be their spiritual descendents. History. Inspiration. Energy. Mission.

Outside it was a cold, early spring evening. But it was warm inside as a couple of dozen members of my parish gathered to share a covered dish supper and afterward learn about the fire that destroyed our previous church building. The meal was good, too good (as usual), and we were all mellow, jovial, and not any more focused than ever as we started sharing about the fire of December

3, 1944. Why didn't we rebuild there? How many buildings have we had over the years? Five? Where were they? So one thing led to another and finally the facts emerged. We have had five church buildings, the previous four having burned to the ground, and not once had the new building been built on the previous site. Why not? Quarrels with neighbors, ha ha? Maybe we never owned the land! Then slowly it dawned on us. The first building built in the late 1700's was on the site of the original settlement. Decades later the town hall and grinding mills were built nearer to the fishing harbors. So there the church relocated after fire razed the first building. Half a century later the breakwater was finished, making the first permanent harbor. So there was the church rebuilt when fire struck again. And so on. Every church building built by our parish was erected in the center of the social life of our community. In the history of our buildings, we came to understand not only who we are as a parish, but also who we always have been. We are the church in location, in island life, and in mission, which is in touch with the center of community life. That one realization reconfirms our self-understanding, sets it in the context of centuries, and motivates us to be who we are. In our history we have found our identity clarified. History. Identity. Energy. Mission.

The heritage of the parish can also provide a lever for a movement forward in faithfulness and ministry. David Ray, small church pastor and author of *Small Churches Are the Right Size*[3], tells of the time his former parish in Warwick, Massachusetts, literally rummaged around in the attic of their "house" church. (Their church building was an old colonial house.) The congregation was in the midst of debating whether to add a sanctuary wing with room for Sunday School classes and community activities. Then, Dueteronomy-like, the documents regarding acquisition of the original building were discovered. It was found that behind the purchase of the house decades earlier had been the intention to use it, not only for worship, but especially to service the community! This truth from their past gave precedent and therefore legitimacy to their present concern to build for more effective ministry to the community. So build they did.

Some of the most effective leadership acts a small church pastor can perform are to become a history buff, read up on the struggle of faith of the parish, sit at the feet of some of the elder members, and play "Remember when. . . ." Initially this may seem like wasted time to a young, energetic, ambitious pastor, but it is in reality time well spent. It will provide the pieces of the puzzle which can be assembled at the point at which God calls the parish forward.

Effective small church leaders will not use bold, new paint, or pie-in-the-sky visions of the New Jerusalem (about to fall on our heads), or Babble on about a Bright New Tomorrow. They will speak quietly about who we are on the basis of who we always have been, about how we can become even more of who we are, about what was good about the "good old days," about how we can keep that good alive in our midst today.

3. Putting a Face on It

In the basement of a small church in Hope, Rhode Island, there is a scale model of a well, complete with roof and bucket. It is labeled "Ronnie's Well" and within the well opening were many coins and bills. My curiosity aroused, I inquired, "What's this?" "Oh," came the reply. "The Peace Corps has a project to dig wells to provide usable water for certain villages in a remote section of Africa where water is scarce. So far we've raised hundreds of dollars through collections and projects and donations to help buy the equipment needed for the wells." Well, that explained the model well and the money, but why was this small group of people so highly committed to a project half way around the globe—a project and a need so remote that virtually no one had ever heard of it. "Oh, that's 'cause of Ronnie. He told us all about it." I was apparently more obtuse than usual that day because I still didn't get it. "Who's Ronnie?"

> Oh, Ronnie is a young man who grew up in our church. His family is very active. After college he wanted to do something for others so he joined the Peace Corps. His assignment was these wells. He wrote us letters and sent pictures explaining his work. You could just sense how important it was to him and the people in the villages to get these wells working. So we've been sending him as much money as we can raise ever since. We think God is really using Ronnie.

My heart warmed once I grasped what it was all about.

That evening I reflected more on the little model well with the money tucked into it. The need was there with or without the Peace Corps. The Peace Corps was there with or without Ronnie. Yet, could you imagine a small church responding to such a need without the Ronnie connection? I can't. There are thousands of third world villages across our globe with needs as compelling, but how many churches do you know working so hard to minister to even one of them? What would a pastor or mission-encourager have to do to actualize such a response? One could hardly conceive of a scenario apart from a Ronnie.

What did Ronnie do for that small group of Christians, struggling to keep the church doors open themselves, that released compassion and caring, effort and resources? Ronnie put a face on the need. He personalized it. No longer were the villagers faceless unknowns. Now they were people named and described, and so obviously cared about by Ronnie. We care about Ronnie. Ronnie cares about them. Therefore we care about them. Ronnie brought them into the tribe. Ronnie appealed to the church's convenantal bonds. There is no anticipation of quid pro quo. The good Christians of Hope are doing what is right to do. They are caring for their own. Ronnie, by his life and love, has made a village half way around the world a part of the relational network of that small church. The typical small church will not respond except perfunctorily to impersonal, data-fied, remote needs. To them mission begins and ends at home. By this I mean that needs which have a claim on us to respond are perceived as personal, actual, close at hand, a disruption in the well-being of the community. This is what motivates a response—not abstract, theoretical, remote, and statistically-defined needs.

Churches with a "global-consciousness" may be able to motivate response on the basis of the objective extent of human need across the world. Churches with "tribal-consciousness" are very seldom able to do so. Here a different strategy must be employed. Instead of bringing the church into the need, the need must be brought into the church. Effective small church leaders will find ways to put a face on the need regarding which they feel God is calling the church to respond. This must be done with care. (People's feelings and dignity must not be sacrificed.) But it is not impossible. After all, if a need has no face, whose need is it?

There are many ways to personalize need. 1) Describe the situation in people terms. Our deacons have been invited to contribute to a local shelter for homeless women for years with no observable response. But when the situation of two families that benefited and some that could not be served due to financial constraints was communicated, their hearts were touched.

2) Establish Relationships. Go and visit. Or bring someone into the life of your congregation. Our parish's support of our State's Hispanic work was formal and uninspired. But since one of our parishioners has worshipped with the Hispanic Church and their pastor has chatted with us over a covered dish supper, our people are spontaneously coming up with ways to help "Francisco." The number of unemployed Hispanics in our state is a sad statistic to which we have no idea how to respond. But we know how to befriend people. Francisco is now our friend. We are pleased to stand be-

hind him, hear news of his work, and support his ministry as we can.

3) Start at home. Sometimes "Mission begins at home" is an excuse to do little or nothing. But what's wrong with inviting people to put their money where their mouth is? Is it better than lamenting the lack of global mission concern and so doing nothing at all? Find out who's hurting in the parish. Who needs a job, a minor repair, money for medicine, a visit from a live body? A group from a Presbyterian church in Pennsylvania working with the Habitat for Humanity program asked if they could do home repairs for our elderly and/or impoverished. I didn't know, but I would find out. A deacon and I visited ten homes, asking permission and looking for needs. And we found 'em! My eyes were opened to the needs right on my doorstep. Now our men have started a "Helping Hands" program to continue to work on these necessary repairs.

4) Expand horizons. Once mission becomes a patterned behavior, its object can be broadened. My island parish was very insular in outlook, especially regarding mission, when I first arrived. The number of families who regularly contributed to our denominational mission program could be counted on one hand with a couple fingers left over. The concern was for our own only. So we developed ways to further help our own: the Mary D Fund (for energy relief), Project Harvest Share (distributing excess garden produce to shut-ins), and the Second Wind Luncheons (for the elderly). As mission activity became more comfortable, it began to expand. A SERRV (third-world handcrafts) table was started and I was thrilled to hear from our mission committee that we had over $1000 in sales last year. And we have half a dozen people talking about a retreat/mission trip to a church a few towns away to help out with a building repair project! Unimaginable behavior twelve years go. But as we got into mission, mission got into us.

4. Arrange an Accident

One of the characteristics of folk ways is that no one knows who originated them. They just happened. There is something "right" about this. What we do is in the order of things, it is not something that someone invented. A preplanned, rational program, proposed and promoted by the pastor or other upstart, is seldom incorporated directly into the life of the tribe. In the face of this dynamic how can a small church leader proceed? A shift in focus is required. One must move away from the logical and rational approach, and let life provide the impetus to faithfulness. I heard of a family who

lived (in material marginality and spiritual surfeit) by the side of the
river. They gardened and gathered fire wood. But primarily they
looked to the river—not in order to plan a way to build a bridge
over it—but because the "stuff" of their life floated down stream
awaiting only their reaching out and appropriating it for their use
and benefit. I submit that the reason why we don't "mine" life is a
weakness of faith, and a limitation of vision. Rather, we feel more in
control if we are planning and programming. Control and faithfulness are not the same, though.

Life's interruptions are filled with God's intentions. John A. Hostetler, in his interesting book on *Amish Society*[4] (It is my belief—
and so Hostetler argues—that Amish society is an example of a folk
society in our time and place) describes the effects of two "accidents" on the understanding and behavior of that closed and tight
society:

> Chance, or what might be called accidental happenings, also
> have the effect of altering traditional behavior patterns. In Ohio,
> two young robbers whose vehicle was stalled in a ditch entered
> a farm house home after dark on the evening of July 18, 1957,
> and in the course of events shot the father, Amishman Paul Cob-
> lentz. One of the young men, Cleo Peters, was given the death
> sentence. Many Amish people signed petitions urging mercy.
> Nine hours before he was scheduled to die, Governor William
> O'Neill commuted the sentence to life imprisonment. Some
> Amish people "became burdened about the spiritual welfare" of
> Cleo Peters. They wrote letters to him and also sent delegations
> to visit him. Discussions and correspondence followed the con-
> version of Mr. Peters. The sad incident was interpreted as an act
> of God, as stated in a letter to the prisoner: "We believe that
> God allowed this to call us back to Him in the work of winning
> souls to His Kingdom." . . . An escaped convict in the midwest
> was discovered working as an Amish farm hand. Without know-
> ing that he was a convict, the Amish befriended him and pre-
> pared to receive him into their church by baptism. At this time
> he confessed his status. Shortly before baptism, someone re-
> ported him to the law officers, who arrested him. He was re-
> turned to prison in the state where he had been convicted only
> to be paroled. Members of the Amish church met him as he left
> the prison and took him to their community. . . . Such unstruc-
> tured incidents, drawn from widely differing communities, have
> the effect of evoking new sentiments or concerns for the out-
> sider. They force the traditional community into thinking on
> new courses of action. When taken as "acts of God," new

courses of action, which would otherwise be resented, are made legitimate.

What could have independently moved the xenophobic Amish culture to befriend and convert an imprisoned murderer? I can conceive of no plan that could accomplish that. But it occurred. In fact, not only did it occur, but it was interpreted as a call from God back to their true selves!

What cannot be planned can be envisioned and orchestrated for God's Kingdom. I was tired of living and worshipping (our sanctuary and parsonage are in the same building) in a century old, drafty, uninsulated, code violating, rundown building. But we struggled to meet general expenses. How could we ever get the vision to repair and renovate our facility? As I mulled over these issues, I got the bill for the church's previous load of fuel oil. It had been one of the coldest years in recent memory. Now it was the last week of December. We were way over budget for heating oil already. It might break our backs to get socked with yet another bill. I could sit on it a week. Create the illusion of fiscal solvency by deferring the expense to the next year. What bad luck! Or. . .or I could look for the blessing in the bill—see it as an instrument of God. The extremely cold year—accidental or providential? I asked the Treasurer to pay the bill immediately. Two weeks later at our annual business meeting the people were shocked by our oil overage. I asked for a committee to investigate installing new windows and insulation. Motion passed without dissent. Six months of homework later the committee proposed a complete renovation and had $23,000 pledged to start us off! It took five years of blood, sweat and tears, but our church building is now renovated and up to code! That one unplanned, oversize fuel bill moved us as no rational argument could have—an accident is always more motivational in a folk society than an argument!

How many accidents is God sending your way? Are you using them as God intends—a divine catalyst for faithfulness?

5. Creating a Climate of the Possible

If you were to ask the people in your small church which is their favorite Biblical book, the answers would vary. Psalms, would say the poets and pray-ers. Romans, would say the believers. James, would say the doers. Acts, would say the activists. And Job, the bereaved and aggrieved. But I would venture to say that the one book that reflects most nearly the mood of the small church today is Lamentations. Listen to most any conversation among your people. The world isn't what it used to be. The country isn't what it used to be. Farming isn't what it used to be. Our town isn't what it used to be. The neighborhood isn't what it used to be. The church isn't what it used to be. The old gray mayor isn't what he used to be. Lament. Lament. Lament. There is a sadness and a grief in small churches today. It is true things aren't what they used to be. But they never were. I wish God had had enough sense to place me in an age when I could have been happy. . . . Well, ahem, I suppose God did. But happiness is not automatic. There is a very real sense in which we choose happiness. My wife is a wonderful companion for me. She is a great helpmate and fellow traveler along life's journey. Yet she has a couple of idiosyncracies. If I focus on them, the joy goes out of our relationship. I have two good, healthy, happy kids. But sometimes I make my family miserable harassing them for falling short of perfection. I have a wonderful, Christian community of faith. But on occasion I get down on these fine people—when I focus on their lacks instead of their strengths.

For some reason the empty half of the glass, rather than the full half, grabs our attention. And the litanies of lament begin. What would happen if we saw what's right instead of what's wrong. What if we took the Bible seriously: "Rejoice, and again I say, rejoice." "Count it all joy. . . ." How is it that in his epistles Paul, no matter how severe the difficulties he dealt with later on, could always find a number of sincere points of praise with which to begin his communication? Does our leadership start with the good and only then address the improvable? We pray "Thy Kingdom come," but do we rejoice in its little manifestations or lament its absences?

Lament is, I believe, the natural response of people who want to function in a folk society way but who actually find that modern society has moved out from underneath them. The dissonance between the way things are and the way we remember them generates lament. Lament is natural, but it is not healthy. It registers the problem, but it does not release a solution. It paralyzes when it should liberate.

The small church leader has two action options in the face of lament. One is to lead (Moses-like or Pied Piper-like?) the folk society into the modern society. This direction is frequently highly rewarded by one's denomination and held up as "successful." So the rural church becomes the regional church—now offering something for everyone. The single cell social nature of the folk society is replaced by a multi-cell structure. The past is radically denied and a new future is sought. Patterned behavior is jettisoned and rational ministry is enacted.

The second option deals with the dissonance and so the lament by remembering that it has always been a struggle, that many of those qualities which made our memories so meaningful are still present with us, and that ultimately the folk society will triumph since it is the fundamental form of human life together and God's eternal promise! It recalls that the good in the good old days is as much a nostalgic creation as it was actually present.

Certainly there is good in most any situation, but our memory retains the good more than the bad and the difficult. The re-apprehension of the degree of blood, sweat, and tears in the good old days can liberate us and energize us for our struggles today. In the midst of our building remodelling drive which I mentioned earlier, after the first blush of progress, contributions plateaued and enthusiasm lagged. Why weren't we able to do what Dr. Roberts at the turn of the century could do when the church was really strong? "Huh," said ninety-five-year-old Gladys. "Sure, Dr. Roberts got a lot done. But it wasn't easy. Every year he'd have to go up and down the main street asking every proprietor for a donation. Some of them he never got a nickel out of, either. Some would give a wagon of coal. That's how the church stayed in the black!" Gladys chuckled warmly. But in those words I gained renewed resolve. Even in "the Golden Age" of our church it was touch and go. Even then it was a struggle. Somehow that brought my current struggle down to manageable proportions. What we struggle over may vary, but that we struggle is constant.

"Would you, too, leave me?" Jesus asked his disciples. "Where would we go? You have the words of life," Peter answered. Sometimes I get disgusted and discouraged by the forces at work in our community. Sometime I weary of the repetitive struggles of my little parish. At those times I direct myself to think very seriously about moving to some place better. I give it a lot of thought and I come up with the same conclusion that the Alcoholics Anonymous program does: there is no such thing as a geographic solution. The search for some place better helps me to focus on what I "have" currently: quality of life, ecological harmony, depth of personal relationships, a role to play in the community, job security, etc., etc. I have sunk my roots here. The winds of change make it harder to blossom and bear fruit, but the soil is still rich and the sun warm. If I give myself to those realities, there is still plenty of satisfaction to be gained. It is harder for folk society people to do things from conviction than it was maybe a generation or two ago to do the same thing "naturally." But if we live out our peoplehood, it will be satisfying. And time is on our side. Material wealth, abundance of energy, and technological progress allow humankind to remake the world in our image. This rational world, the world of our minds and egos, is very powerful. People desire this world—it attracts like a magnet. But they can't actually live there. It is the personal world, the world of the small church, the folk society which is finally meaningful and satisfying. Someday we will run out of cheap fuels and humankind will have to learn to live simply, on a small scale and in harmony with nature again. Then it may well be the small churches who by their very life and nature will be salvific for society at large.

But in the meantime? It is not productive to sit around waiting for the judgment day. In the meantime we can recognize our strengths, realize that at least a glimmer of eternity is embodied in our life together, and praise God for who we are and what we do. If we take this posture, we are much more likely to be faithful to God's calling than if we preoccupy ourselves with our weaknesses. A little rejoicing is infinitely better than a lot of lamenting.

In I Corinthians Paul writes that God calls into beings those who were nothings. In the eyes of the world, even sometimes in the eyes of the denomination, the small church is a nothing. Small church people come to think of themselves similarly. Part of ministry, part of God's salvation, is to be called into being. Call your congregation into being. Acknowledge their strengths, emphasize what they have, not what they lack. After all, only those who first "are" are active and improving.

6. If All Else Fails, Pray!

Sometimes the best way to get something done is not to try to get anything done at all. This approach is, of course, nonsense to those who have bought into the values of corporate Ameria. What good is someone who doesn't aim to get anything done? For these people, they are the actors and the world around them is acted upon. It is a little more intricate for the Christian, though. God is the Actor. The world evidences these actions. We are to discern God's activity and coordinate ourselves with it. It is even more intricate still in the folk society. Leadership activity is likely to be resisted, as Moses found out: "Who appointed *you* lord and master over *us*?"

I distinctly remember being burned by this latter dynamic. I was the spokesperson for a town appointed committee. We had done an incredible amount of homework, marshalled our data and arguments, and attempted to persuade our Town Fathers to budget monies for improved medical service in the upcoming fiscal year. I presented a case which was thoroughly convincing, at least to me.

But instead of unanimous support our committee was raked over the coals! Finally, they decided to defer the decision. I sat down stunned. Next, the town road worker submitted his budget request "Do you want us to approve this increase?" A shrug. "Whatever you'd like to do." " Do you really need this much money?" "Nope. Only if you want the roads tended." "Why should we pass this now?" "So I can go home and watch the rest of the Red Sox game." Request approved! A townsperson, noticing my dazed look, took pity on me. "You know where you went wrong, Rev.? You acted like you really wanted your request approved. You shudda played it cool like John. If they think you're pushing, they wonder what you're trying to put over on them." This dynamic is operative in the small church, too. To get too intense about one's agenda is to in- hibit, not increase the likelihood of the desired outcome.

Rather, it is sometimes better to do nothing. I think this was the real genius of our Men's Prayer Breakfast. (I realized afterward!) We had no explicit agenda, except to share and pray. As we got more comfortable (realized that no one was going to shove his agenda down another's throat), the sharing deepened. As the sharing deep- ened, individual and corporate concerns began to be voiced and clarified. As we became more sensitive to our own felt needs, we discerned a certain set about which we could do something. Out of that realization came ministry. Not necessarily a ministry I would have chosen, but the right one nonetheless. Not out of any plan- ning, nor out of "being intentional," nor out of any goal-setting, but out of what God had put in our hearts emerged our outreach re- sponse.

In folk societies the generational kinship structure is comple- mented by a secondary but very important social clustering. In cer- tain cultures it is gender defined, in others it is age bracketed, or in others it is like a "club" with strict rules. These associations play an important role in the life of the tribe. They accomplish certain spe- cific functions or redress social imbalances, i.e., they have their own ministry though they are structured for form not function. The en- ergy released in these subgroups is an important factor for leader- ship. Wesley structured this in "class meetings." Duncan McIntosh talks about creating "hot spots" for change—a handful of like- minded people within the whole congregation. Paul Cho champions "cell groups." The power released when people get together to be, pray, and share is tremendous, if not necessarily controllable. But the effective small church leader recognizes that God, not she or he, is in control. Gather some open-hearted folk together and just see what God will do!

Summary of Actions

In the two preceding sections I have attempted to lift up half a
dozen attitudes and types of actions that I believe to be helpful to a
small church leader who desires to be more effective. It should be
noted that these are tools, not directives, nor blueprints. These tools
are not meant to define ministry in a local situation. The content of
your ministry, the direction God is calling you in is not specifiable
by me—only you in expectancy and faithfulness can determine it.
These tools are meant to facilitate the process of embodying God's
calling in your situation. On the other hand, these tools are not
meant to be a step-by-step guide to effective leadership, removing
from you any necessity for thought, prayer and sensitivity. Rather,
they are meant to be simply tools, approaches, which when brought
to bear on the particulars of your situation may help you realize
God's intention by working with, not against, the social nature of
the small church.

With these cautions in mind, let us review the six action applica-
tions I have put forward.

1. Horse or Cart? The small church is primarily a reflexive not a
reflective entity. It knows by experiencing, more than by analyzing.
In doing more than discussing can a small church determine
whether it is comfortable in proceeding. Effective small church
leaders allow experience as an input into important discussions.
Two strategies which embody this dynamic are the trial period and
a step-by-step approach.

2. The Good Old Days. Small churches are motivated more by
their heritage than by a vision for the future. Effective small church
leaders familiarize themselves with their church's heritage—rum-
mage around in the attic of the church's memories. This expands
the leader's understanding and communicates a positive regard of
the people. But it also gives the small church leader points of lever-
age when movement is required. It allows the parish to move forward by looking backward!

3. Putting a Face On It. Small churches are motivated to respond to relational, not abstract realities. Needs that are tangible,
close at hand, personal and within the relational network of the
congregation can be registered and responded to. Four ways to
move in this direction are to 1) describe issues in people terms,
2) establish relationships, 3) start at home, and 4) expand horizons.

4. Arrange an Accident. Small church folk are more at home
with Fate than intentionality. They respond better to an accident

than to an action plan. This may frustrate those leaders who have to have the church do their particular thing. But it works out fine for those who are looking to do God's thing! Effective small church leaders take their action cues from particulars of the situation and they know how to shape them to catch the attention and energy of their congregations.

5. Creating a Climate of the Possible. Small churches by society's values are often considered marginal, non-existent. Yet only those who exist can act and progress. Effective small church leaders communicate the reality and potency of their people by acknowledging their value in God's eyes, their actual strengths, and the Christ-like qualities which they embody. Thus becoming "somebody" they are more ready to grow into the fullness of Christ.

6. If All Else Fails, Pray! Few today consider prayer action. Yet a handful of open, concerned Christians meeting to pray can catch fire and really brighten up the corner where they are. It was those few timid souls meeting behind closed doors upon whom the fire of the Holy Spirit fell. The world has not been the same since.

CHAPTER VI

Conclusion

Radically different tools are needed to build an igloo and a highrise condominium. They are each capable of becoming "home," but the differences are important if each is to become livable. So with the church. The church may be the church, if we are speaking abstractly and theologically. But the differences are more important if each type of local church is to be built up into our spiritual home. This book has been concerned with one type of local church which differs markedly from other types. We have focused on the small church and claimed that it can best be understood as a contemporary manifestation of the timeless social type known as the "folk society." We have claimed that small church people live in their "world"—a world which differs significantly from the world of our society's predominant culture. We have sought to get inside this world, to feel it and see what it looks like. We have then put forward understandings and behaviors that small church leaders can utilize toward greater effectiveness in this world. Not all small churches are in this world. Some large churches are. No small church sees things exactly as described here. Nevertheless, I believe that the essential characteristics of this world have been put forward and that this picture of this world can be utilized to advantage by those who desire to see the Kingdom of God realized in the small church. That is what this book is finally about. It is an invitation to stop kicking against the goads and enter the world of the small church. To minister therein on its own terms and to realize just how much of the Kingdom is there. God bless you in your journey.

Chapter II

1. Paul S. Minear, *Images of the Church in the New Testament* (Philadelphia: The Westminster Press, 1960).
2. Robert Redfield, "The Folk Society," *The American Journal of Sociology*, (LII:4), January, 1947.
3. Harold Moore, "The Pastor as Family Therapist," *The Five Stones* (Vol. 2), Spring, 1987.
4. Conversation with author.
5. Dolores Curran, *Traits of a Healthy Family* (San Francisco: Harper and Row, 1983), pp. 23-24.
6. Carl S. Dudley, *Unique Dynamics of the Small Church* (Washington, DC: The Alban Institute, 1977), p. 6.
7. Arlin J. Rothauge, *Sizing Up a Congregation* (New York: Seabury Professional Services, 1983).
8. Lyle E. Schaller, *Looking in the Mirror* (Nashville: Abingdon Press, 1984).

Chapter III

1. Redfield, Op. Cit., p. 301.
2. Elenore Smith Bowen, *Return to Laughter* (New York: Harper and Row, 1954), pp. 274-275.

Chapter IV

1. Elman R. Service, "The Ghosts of Our Ancestors," *Primitive Worlds: People Lost in Time*, (Washington, DC: The National Geographic Society, 1973), p. 9-10.
2. Redfield, Op. Cit., p. 293.
3. Ibid., p. 298.
4. Ibid., pp. 299-300.
5. Ibid., p. 300.
6. Ibid., p. 303.
7. Bowen, Op. Cit., pp. 74-75.
8. Ibid., p. 223.

Chapter V

1. Jackson W. Carroll, *Small Churches Are Beautiful*, (San Francisco: Harper and Row, 1977).

2. Arthur Kinoy, *The Real Mystery of Block Island*, Block Island Historical Society, Block Island, RI, 1961.

3. David R. Ray, *Small Churches Are the Right Size*, (New York: The Pilgrim Press, 1982).

4. John A. Hostetler, *Amish Society*, 3rd Edition, (Baltimore: The Johns Hopkins University Press, 1980), pp. 285-286.

The Alban Institute:
an invitation to membership

The Alban Institute, begun in 1979, believes that the congregation is essential to the task of equipping the people of God to minister in the church and the world. A multi-denominational membership organization, the Institute provides on-site training, educational programs, consulting, research, and publishing for hundreds of churches across the country.

The Alban Institute invites you to be a member of this partnership of laity, clergy, and executives—a partnership that brings together people who are raising important questions about congregational life and people who are trying new solutions, making new discoveries, finding a new way of getting clear about the task of ministry. The Institute exists to provide you with the kinds of information and resources you need to support your ministries.

Join us now and enjoy these benefits:

CONGREGATIONS, The Alban Journal, a highly respected journal published six times a year, to keep you up to date on current issues and trends.

Inside Information, Alban's quarterly newsletter, keeps you informed about research and other happenings around Alban. Available to members only.

Publications Discounts:

☐ 15% for Individual, Retired Clergy, and Seminarian Members
☐ 25% for Congregational Members
☐ 40% for Judicatory and Seminary Executive Members

Discounts on Training and Education Events

Write our Membership Department at the address below or call us at (202) 244-7320 for more information about how to join The Alban Institute's growing membership, particularly about Congregational Membership in which 12 designated persons receive all benefits of membership.

The Alban Institute, Inc.
4125 Nebraska Avenue, NW
Washington, DC 20016